OSPREY AIRCRAFT OF TI

More Bf 109 Aces
of the Russian Front

SERIES EDITOR: TONY HOLMES

OSPREY AIRCRAFT OF THE ACES® • 76

More Bf 109 Aces of the Russian Front

John Weal

OSPREY
PUBLISHING

First published in Great Britain in 2007 by Osprey Publishing,
Midland House, West Way, Botley, Oxford OX2 0PH, UK
44-02 23rd St, Suite 219, Long Island City, NY 11101, USA
Email: info@ospreypublishing.com

Transferred to digital print on demand 2011

First published 2007
3rd impression 2008

Printed and bound by Cadmus Communications, USA

A CIP catalogue record for this book is available from the British Library

ISBN: 978 1 84603 177 9

Edited by Tony Holmes
Page design by Tony Truscott
Cover Artwork by Mark Postlethwaite
Aircraft Profiles by John Weal
Index by Alan Thatcher
Originated by PDQ Digital Media Solutions

Acknowledgements
The author wishes to thank the following individuals for their invaluable help in providing photographs and other material
for his book – Michael Denley, Mark Gordon Forbes, Jerry Scutts, Robert Simpson, Herren Rolf Beckmann, Mathias Deger,
the late Heinz Ewald, Manfred Griehl, Gerhard Krämer, Norbert Hannig, Walter Matthiesen and Axel Paul.

The Woodland Trust
Osprey Publishing is supporting the Woodland Trust, the UK's leading woodland conservation charity, by funding the
dedication of trees.

www.ospreypublishing.com

Front cover
22 June 1941, and in a scene re-enacted hundreds of times during the opening days and weeks of Operation *Barbarossa*,
low-flying Soviet bombers – in this case Tupolev SB-2s – strive desperately to halt the invading German ground forces.
The Red Air Force bomber formations, more often than not completely devoid of fighter cover, suffered enormous losses
at the hands of the Luftwaffe's Bf 109s. Many future semi-centurions of the Russian Front opened their score sheets
during actions such as this.

The pilot of 6./JG 54's 'Yellow 4', depicted here in this specially commissioned artwork by Mark Postlethwaite, was
Leutnant Horst Hannig, whose first victory was just one of 11 Tupolev bombers claimed by II./JG 54 during a 25-minute
engagement close to the Lithuanian border. 'The Ivans were sitting ducks', Hannig later told a war reporter. 'They didn't
stand a chance without their own fighters to protect them', he concluded.

During his 18 months' service on the Russian front, Horst Hannig would claim 90 Soviet aircraft destroyed. Early in
1943, the then Oberstleutnant Hannig would be appointed *Staffelkapitän* of 2./JG 2 'Richthofen' on the Channel coast.
He was killed in action during an engagement with RAF Spitfires near Caen on 15 May 1943, by which point he had
boosted his tally to 98 victories. (*Cover artwork by Mark Postlethwaite*)

CONTENTS

BARBAROSSA

The most commonly accepted definition of an ace, and the one used throughout by *Osprey's Aircraft of the Aces* series, is any pilot with five or more aerial kills to his credit. By this yardstick, or indeed any other, the greatest assemblage of aces ever involved in a single campaign came from the ranks of the Luftwaffe *Jagdgruppen* engaged against the Soviet Red Air Force between June 1941 and May 1945.

In the first volume of this two-part work (*Osprey Aircraft of the Aces 37 – Bf 109 Aces of the Russian Front*), an attempt was made briefly to describe the background, and explain the unique set of circumstances, that led up to the air war in the east. This conflict gave many German fighter pilots, both veteran and tyro alike, the chance to amass huge scores against their numerically superior communist opponents. In its early stages at least, the conflict was very much a one-sided contest fought against an ill-prepared, inadequately trained, poorly equipped and badly led enemy. Many months would pass before the Soviets rectified these shortcomings, and before their sheer weight of numbers finally, and irrevocably, tipped the balance in favour of the Red Air Force.

The increasingly bitter four-year struggle against the USSR's land and naval air forces would result in the emergence of literally hundreds of Luftwaffe five-victory aces. But limitations of space meant that the emphasis in the first of these two volumes had to be focussed primarily on the top 75 *Experten* of the Russian front – those illustrious individuals who racked up totals of 100 or more Soviet aircraft destroyed.

Almost exactly twice that number of German fighter pilots (some 154 in all), however, are known to have achieved scores ranging from 50 to 99 against the Russians. These 'semi-centurions', as one Luftwaffe historian has labelled them, should in no way be regarded as second stringers. They were all highly proficient and successful pilots. To put matters into perspective, each and every one of them surpassed – many, in fact, more than doubled – the numbers of victories claimed by the leading British and American aces of World War 2. Apart from Germany, only four other nations produced fighter pilots with scores of 50+, namely the Soviet Union, Japan, Finland and Rumania.

The Luftwaffe's Russian front semi-centurions fall into two distinct categories. First came those whose Soviet kills formed but a part, albeit usually a major one, of their totals. Among this group can be found a number of well-known names, such as the irrepressible Heinz 'Pritzl' Bär, whose roller-coaster career resulted in 220 victories, 96 of them claimed against the Red Air Force. Another is Walter Dahl, more closely associated with *Sturm* operations in Defence of the Reich, but whose final total of 128 included 77 kills in the east, with 25 over Stalingrad alone.

Unlike Bär and Dahl, Günther Lützow did not survive the war. But 85 of the 103 victories he had claimed prior to being reported missing in a Me 262 jet fighter just a fortnight before Germany surrendered had been achieved while leading JG 3 during the first 13 months of the campaign against the Soviet Union.

There were two types of Russian front 50+ *Experten*. First, there were the well-known names whose victories against the Soviets were just a chapter in their long and often illustrious wartime careers. One such was Hauptmann Heinz Bär, who claimed 96 of his 220 kills in the east . . .

The second group consists of those pilots whose kills were *all* scored on the Russian front. Given the anonymous nature of much of the action against the Red Air Force, and the scant coverage that has been afforded the air war in the east over the six decades since hostilities ceased, the names of many of these latter *Experten* may be less familiar – possibly even completely unknown – to most people today. They played an integral and important part in the titanic struggle between the air forces of the Third Reich and the USSR, however, and, in so doing, have earned themselves a legitimate place in the annals of military aviation.

As in the earlier campaigns against Poland, the Low Countries and France, Hitler's invasion of Stalinist Russia opened in true *Blitzkrieg* fashion with heavy air attacks on the enemy's forward airfields. The results exceeded all expectations. By last light on 22 June 1941 – the opening day of Operation *Barbarossa* – it was estimated that some 1500 Soviet aircraft had been destroyed on the ground. A further 322 had been shot down, some 80 percent of which had fallen to Bf 109 fighters. One source gives the exact number of kills credited to the *Jagdwaffe* on 22 June 1941 as 264!

The fortunes of individual *Jagdgruppen* varied widely, as so often happened on the Russian front. Collective totals on that first day of *Barbarossa* ranged from no victories at all to a staggering 36 (amassed, together with 28 enemy machines destroyed on the ground, by Hauptmann Wolf-Dietrich Wilcke's III./JG 53 – the highest daily score by any Luftwaffe *Jagdgruppe* in the war to date).

The 20 *Jagdgruppen* with which the Luftwaffe embarked upon the invasion of the Soviet Union were somewhat unevenly deployed along the three sectors of the main fighting front (for a full listing including bases, COs, and strengths, see page 85 of *Aircraft of the Aces 37*).

On the northern sector, forming part of *Luftflotte* 1 (the air fleet tasked with supporting Army Group North's drive through the Baltic states to Leningrad), was a single *Jagdgeschwader* – JG 54, commanded by Major Hannes Trautloft and bolstered temporarily by the attached II./JG 53.

Trautloft's reinforced command was credited with 45 victories on the opening day of *Barbarossa*. Accompanying II./JG 54 on a bomber escort mission against enemy airfields just over the border in Soviet-occupied Lithuania, the *Kommodore* himself was able to claim one of them to add to his existing score of eight enemy aircraft destroyed. Although Trautloft's own *Friedrich* was severely damaged in the action, he managed to nurse it back to base at Trakehnen, where he pulled off a successful belly landing.

Another five machines of the Red Air Force would fall to Trautloft's guns before the month of June was out. He was a towering presence, both physically and figuratively, in the wartime *Jagdwaffe*. But he was rightfully acclaimed more for his qualities of leadership than for his seeking personal aggrandisement and an impressive individual score. Thus, by the time he finally relinquished command of JG 54 in the summer of 1943 to join the staff of *General der Jagdflieger* Adolf Galland, Hannes Trautloft's own Russian front tally was still five short of 50.

Three pilots of II./JG 54 with whom Trautloft had flown on 22 June 1941 would, however, go on to become semi-centurions. Leutnant Horst Hannig opened his scoreboard with a single kill on this first day of the

... then there were those whose victories were *all* achieved on the Russian front. Despite being in the majority, few of their names are remembered today. Leutnant Ulrich Wöhnert, for example, who ended the war with 86 kills – more than *double* the score of the leading RAF fighter ace – remains all but unknown

campaign against Russia, while Oberleutnant Carl Sattig and Hauptmann Franz Eckerle each claimed one apiece – their second and fifth victories respectively.

Also engaged over the Lithuanian border regions, I/JG 54's collective total of a dozen Soviet machines shot down included a trio for Hauptmann Reinhard Seiler, thereby doubling his current score to six. In contrast, the pilots of III./JG 54 were credited with only six between them. But among these were a pair of Polikarpov fighters which provided a first for Leutnant Hans-Joachim Heyer and a second for Unteroffizier Eugen-Ludwig Zweigart.

Meanwhile, in the southern sector, *Luftflotte* 4 was fielding two *Jagdgeschwader* whose job was to cover Army Group South's advance into the Ukraine. On the left-hand flank, based around Hostynne, in the southeastern corner of German-occupied Poland, were the three *Gruppen* of Major Günther Lützow's JG 3.

As with JG 54 up in East Prussia, it was the *Geschwaderkommodore* himself who claimed the *Stab's* sole success of 22 June 1941. The Soviet fighter was victory number 19 for 'Franzl' Lützow, who was another ex-*Legion Condor* veteran like Trautloft, but one who was already wearing the Knight's Cross (awarded at the height of the Battle of Britain for his then 15 kills).

Eight of the 24 enemy aircraft downed by Lützow's three component *Gruppen* on the opening day of *Barbarossa* were credited to I./JG 3, but none of these fell to future semi-centurions. II. *Gruppe's* 15 kills, however, included firsts for both Oberleutnant Walther Dahl and Leutnant Hans Fuss, while Oberleutnant Franz Beyer and Feldwebel Alfred Heckmann added to the three victories that each already had under his belt. III./JG 3 were far less successful. At a cost of two *Friedrichs* lost and five damaged,

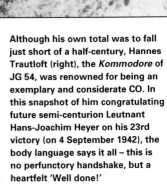

Although his own total was to fall just short of a half-century, Hannes Trautloft (right), the *Kommodore* of JG 54, was renowned for being an exemplary and considerate CO. In this snapshot of him congratulating future semi-centurion Leutnant Hans-Joachim Heyer on his 23rd victory (on 4 September 1942), the body language says it all – this is no perfunctory handshake, but a heartfelt 'Well done!'

One of the many who opened his score sheet (with a Tupolev SB-2) on the first day of *Barbarossa* was II./JG 54's Leutnant Horst Hannig. Here, 11 months and a further 47 victories later, he poses happily with his newly awarded Knight's Cross

they were able to achieve just one victory. But the I-15 claimed by 7. *Staffel's* Unteroffizier Helmut Rüffler on 22 June 1941 was to be just the first of his 76 Russian front victories.

To the south of JG 3, down in Rumania, were two *Gruppen* of Major Bernhard Woldenga's JG 77, together with the subordinated I.(J)/LG 2. Equipped predominantly with Bf 109Es, and tasked primarily with ground-attack sorties, the units' combined total of Red Air Force fighters shot down numbered only 15. Among the claimants were Oberleutnants Walther Höckner and Kurt Ubben, of II. and III./JG 77 respectively, both of whom were in the early stages of their scoring careers.

The *Gruppenkommandeur* of I.(J)/LG 2, Hauptmann Herbert Ihlefeld, by contrast, was yet another 'old hand' who had fought in the Spanish Civil War, where he had accounted for seven Republican aircraft. He too was sporting the Knight's Cross, which he had received in September 1940 after attaining 21 victories. Since then he had almost doubled that figure. The I-16 *Rata* that Herbert Ihlefeld brought down in the opening minutes of *Barbarossa* – one of a trio claimed by his *Gruppe* – was the *Kommandeur's* 37th kill of World War 2.

The most southerly of all the Bf 109s ranged against the Soviet Union were the *Friedrichs* of Major Gotthard Handrick's III./JG 52. This *Gruppe's* commitments were purely defensive, however – the protection of the Rumanian oilfields around Ploesti and the oil terminal port of Constanza, on the Black Sea coast. But despite several Red Air Force bombing raids against the latter target during the first 48 hours of the campaign in the east, Handrick's pilots were unable to claim a single kill.

It was a different matter entirely on the central sector. This was the area from which the main land assault against the Soviet Union was launched, with two massive armoured formations striking eastwards along parallel

In contrast to Leutnant Horst Hannig's SB-2, the I-16 that Hauptmann Herbert Ihlefeld, *Kommandeur* of I.(J)/LG 2, downed on 22 June 1941 was his 37th kill of the war to date. Caught in relaxed mood at Jassy, in Rumania, in mid-July, Ihlefeld is sat in front of his Bf 109E. Note that the fighter's scoreboard on the rudder totals 46 kills, revealing just how busy its pilot has been since the opening day of *Barbarossa*

axes of advance towards a single objective – Moscow. To cover this twin-pronged attack, it was also the area where nearly half of all the Luftwaffe *Jagdgruppen* (nine out of the twenty) engaged in *Barbarossa* were concentrated. And between them these nine would account for 182 enemy aircraft, or almost 70 percent of all the Red Air Force machines shot down on the first day of the campaign in the east.

The *Jagdgeschwader* charged with supporting the left-hand wing of the drive on Moscow was Major Wolfgang Schellmann's JG 27, which consisted at this time of its own subordinate II. and III. *Gruppen*, plus the temporarily attached II./JG 52 and III./JG 53.

JG 27's units would not remain in the east long enough to produce any really high scorers against the Soviets. Their rise to fame would come after they were transferred to the North African theatre. But two future semi-centurions of II./JG 52 claimed their first kills on 22 June 1941. Oberfähnrich Waldemar Semelka dispatched an I-15 fighter in mid-morning and Oberleutnant Rudolf Resch was credited with the *Gruppe's* 16th, and final, success of the day – a twin-engined Tupolev SB-2 light bomber, which Luftwaffe pilots often erroneously referred to as 'Martins' – late in the afternoon.

It was the other *Gruppe* currently operating under JG 27, Hauptmann Wolf-Dietrich Wilcke's III./JG 53, that was responsible for the highest collective tally of the day with 36 Red Air Force machines shot down. Of this number, only two need concern us here. These were a pair of 'I-17' fighters – brought down within three minutes of each other – that took future *Experte* Oberleutnant Friedrich-Karl Müller's score to 12.

Berlin-born Friedrich-Karl 'Tutti' Müller who served with both JGs 53 and 3, and who should not be confused with nightfighter ace Friedrich-Karl 'Nasen' Müller, was featured, and listed, in Osprey's *Aircraft of the Aces 37* as having attained 100 Russian front victories. Subsequent research, however, suggests that his successes against the Red Air Force in fact totalled 'only' 87.

Finally, covering the right wing of the armoured advance on Moscow, were the five *Jagdgruppen* that would be involved in some of the heaviest

The losses in men and machines were not completely one-sided, however. IV./JG 51 wrote off two 'Brown 1s' in forced landings away from base during the early stages of *Barbarossa*. The pilots were Otto Steitz and Heinz Bär. The two kill bars just visible on the rudder of this *Friedrich* (immediately aft of the swastika) would seem to suggest that it was the mount of Feldwebel Steitz

Two – or should that really be three? – early Russian front semi-centurions. Hauptmann Karl-Gottfried Nordmann, *Kommandeur* of IV./JG 51 (left), Oberstleutnant Werner Mölders, *Kommodore* of JG 51 (centre), and Major Günther Lützow, *Kommodore* JG 3 (right)

fighting in the opening stages of the campaign. They were divided between two *Geschwaderstäbe*. JG 51 deployed its own I., II., and III. *Gruppen*, while IV./JG 51 was temporarily detached to serve alongside I./JG 53 under the latter's *Stab* JG 53. Between them they would account for 117 enemy aircraft on the opening day of *Barbarossa*, with 28 of this number falling to the guns of future semi-centurions.

The SB-2 claimed by Oberleutnant Hartmann Grasser of *Stab* JG 51, for example, was his eighth victory of the war to date. The *Stab's* four other kills were all credited to the *Kommodore*, Major Werner Mölders. These took the latter's overall total to 72, and were but the first of his 33 confirmed Russian front victories. However, it is strongly rumoured that Mölders achieved many more 'unofficial' kills, particularly after being banned from all further operational flying upon becoming the first fighter pilot in the world to top the 100 mark. Indeed, there is reported evidence in private logbooks and diaries for at least six such unrecognised victories. And it may well be that, among all his other achievements, the legendary Werner Mölders was also a covert Russian front semi-centurion!

No uncertainty surrounds eight of Mölders's pilots who scored during the first day of action against the Soviets, and who would amass 50+ victories in the east. All but five of I./JG 51's 18 successes of 22 June 1941 were credited to such future *Experten*.

Oberleutnant Heinrich Krafft, the *Kapitän* of 3. *Staffel*, doubled his existing score to eight during the course of three separate sorties on this date, while Leutnant Heinz Bär's trio of kills took his total to 20. Two NCO pilots also opened their score sheets – Oberfeldwebel Heinrich Höfemeier was credited with four SB-2s in the space of just six minutes before his own 'White 5' was damaged by return fire from the Soviet bombers and he was himself wounded, while Unteroffizier Herbert Bareuther claimed a single SB-2. Yet another of the seemingly ubiquitous SB-2s gave victory number two to Unteroffizier Wilhelm Theimann, whose only previous claim had been for a Spitfire in November 1940.

Perversely, not a single one of II./JG 51's 28 kills went to a future semi-centurion. III. *Gruppe* fared slightly better in this respect, with three out of its day's collective total of 19 falling to *Kommandeur* Hauptmann Richard Leppla, thereby raising his overall tally to 16. And three pilots of IV./JG 51, currently serving under *Stab* JG 53, were responsible for seven of their *Gruppe's* 23 kills. Oberleutnant Karl-Gottfried Nordmann, the *Kapitän* of 12./JG 51, accounted for four of them (numbers 10 to 13 on his score sheet), with two more constituting the first successes of the war for one of the members of his *Staffel*, 19-year-old Austrian Oberfähnrich Ernst Weismann, and the last taking the personal total of 10./JG 51's Leutnant Bernd Gallowitsch to six.

Lastly, *Stab* and I./JG 53 contained only one future member of the 50+ fraternity among their ranks on 22 June 1941. Another Austrian, Leutnant Walter Zellot opened his scoring with a single I-16 *Rata* downed just beyond the Polish-Soviet frontier in mid-morning.

By the end of the first day of *Barbarossa* there is little doubt that the Luftwaffe had dealt the Red Air Force a grievous blow – grievous, but not fatal. Although it is true that most of the Soviet fighter units based close to the border had effectively been wiped out, the enemy still deployed many hundreds of twin-engined bombers further to the rear. The first retaliatory raids against the invading German ground forces had already been launched by the nearest of these machines during the opening afternoon of the campaign. And many more were being rushed forward to within striking distance of the fighting fronts.

This set the pattern for the early days and weeks of the air war in the east, as wave after wave of unescorted Ilyushins and Tupolevs mounted near suicidal attacks on German armoured spearheads, troop columns and airfields. They were hacked down in their dozens – often whole formations at a time. A diarist (of II./JG 51) left an impression of one such raid;

'On 24 June the Soviets send in their Martin (Tupolev SB-2) bombers to attack the marching columns of infantry. They sweep in very low, really "hedge-hopping". For our fighters it means emergency scramble!

'Whether we want to or not, our fighters have to hedge-hop at the same height as the bombers. Not a very comfortable feeling, knowing that your parachute will be of no use if you take a hit this close to the ground.

'The footsloggers, who are watching the wild chase just above their heads, wave excitedly. We know what this waving means – "Give it to them!"

'Still at zero altitude, the Soviets let fly with all they have at the fast-approaching fighters. They have no other way of defending themselves. The Martin bombers are much too heavy and cumbersome to get drawn into a dogfight.

'Then the fighters are in range. Their fingers on the triggers, the pilots wait for the exact moment to open fire. For many it is the first time they have a real enemy in their sights. They are astonished to discover that

Another to claim his first victory on 22 June 1941 was Leutnant Walter Zellot. With the exception of three RAF fighters downed during I./JG 53's operations against Malta in the first half of 1942, all of Zellot's 84 subsequent successes were achieved against the USSR – the last on 9 September 1942, just 24 hours before his own *Gustav* fell victim to Soviet flak near Stalingrad

Many Luftwaffe fighter pilots cut their operational teeth on Tupolev's twin-engined SB-2 and -3 bombers during the opening stages of the air war in the east. Among the hundreds brought down was this example being inspected by army troops on the central sector

everything they have been taught in theory does actually happen – the bombers burst into flames and soon look more like blazing torches than aircraft.

'Every one of the pilots who lands back at Terespol 20 minutes later (the *Gruppe* had moved forward from Siedlce the previous day) reports shooting down a Soviet bomber.'

II./JG 51's collective total for the day was 16 SB-2s and five Ilyushin DB-3s. Twenty-four hours later the *Gruppe* was back in action over the same area, protecting the ground forces as they advanced along the northern edge of the Pripyet marshes. In three separate engagements during the course of the day its pilots accounted for no fewer than 28 bombers, all of them identified as SB-2s.

Among the claimants during the morning's action involving 5. *Staffel* were Leutnant Hans Strelow, who was credited with his first victory on this date, Unteroffizier Wilhelm Mink, whose brace of bombers took his existing score to four, and Feldwebel Otto Tange, who likewise doubled his existing pre-*Barbarossa* total to six by despatching a trio of the unescorted Tupolevs. All three pilots went on to achieve 60+ Russian front kills. None would survive the war.

Meanwhile, on the southernmost sector of the front, III./JG 52 had finally found a solution to its problems. With *Barbarossa* about to enter its third day, it was the only *Jagdgruppe* on the Russian front to have not yet claimed a single Soviet aircraft destroyed. By this time Axis ground forces had advanced out of Rumania and were already biting deep into western Ukraine. But III./JG 52 was not ordered forward to keep pace with them. It remained in the rear area, protecting the oil terminal of Constanza.

It was not proving an easy job. Lacking any form of early warning system – either human or electronic – the *Gruppe's* pilots were finding it impossible to intercept the Soviet bombers that were flying in from across the Black Sea, attacking their coastal targets and then rapidly retiring back out over open water again.

In an effort to improve the situation, the *Gruppe* rotated a *Staffel* at a time from Bucharest-Pipera and Mizil down to the forward landing ground at Mamaia, right on the coast just a few miles to the north of Constanza. But even this was not enough. It was Oberleutnant Günther Rall, the *Kapitän* of 8./JG 52, who came up with the answer.

Rather than have the entire *Staffel* waiting at readiness at Mamaia for the enemy to come into sight, he ordered a pair of Messerschmitts to patrol out to sea off Constanza to give warning of approaching Soviet bombers. If no aircraft had appeared before the first two fighters began to run low on fuel, they would be relieved on station by a second pair – and so on throughout the day so that a constant watch could be maintained.

This added precaution proved unnecessary. Not long after the first two Bf 109Fs had lifted off from Mamaia's grassy surface and headed out to sea into the eye of the rising sun, the remainder of the *Staffel* – strapped into their cockpits, the engines of their fighters already warmed up – heard an excited shout over the R/T – 'They're coming!'

Within two minutes every machine was in the air and on course to intercept the incoming enemy bombers, which had been identified as the heavier, longer-range Ilyushin Il-3s – the type that provided the backbone of the Soviet Black Sea Fleet's naval air arm.

But the Ilyushins were no match for Rall's pilots. In a running battle lasting little more than half-an-hour, ten of their number were shot down (another was despatched after a further 20-minute chase back out to sea, and a 12th – either a straggler or a single intruder – was brought down some time later by the leader of the next standing patrol).

Among the pilots to claim kills on this morning of 24 June were future half-centurions Unteroffizier Gerhard Köppen and Oberge-freiter Friedrich Wachowiak, both of whom opened their respective accounts with a pair of bombers each. The Soviets attacked again late the following afternoon, and on this occasion the defending fighters from III./JG 52 sent five enemy bombers crashing into the sea off Constanza. Two of these victories launched the careers of yet another pair of semi-centurions by providing the first kills for 7. *Staffel's* Unteroffiziere Edmund 'Paule' Rossmann and Kurt Ratzlaff.

But the *Gruppe's* biggest haul of Russian bombers was claimed early the next morning, 26 June, when they were credited with 18 DB-3s and SB-2s destroyed before 0600 hrs! III./JG 52 had thus brought down a total of 35 enemy raiders in three days, and in so doing had saved the Constanza oil terminal from serious damage. Thereafter, the Soviet attacks tailed off, and there were no further engagements for the remainder of the month. This was through no fault of III./JG 52, which continued to fly its coastal patrols.

All the more puzzling then, the now infamous telegram sent to the *Gruppenkommandeur* early in July by a petulant and ill-informed *Reichsmarschall* Hermann Göring, Commander-in-Chief of the Luftwaffe, enquiring facetiously 'how much longer are the Russians to be allowed into your airspace unhindered?'

Meanwhile, on the land fronts, the last eight days of June 1941 were to see Axis ground forces continuing to advance eastwards almost unimpeded. Having smashed through the Soviets' frontier defences, each of the three main army groups now had their eyes firmly fixed on the next stages along the roads to their ultimate objectives of Leningrad, Moscow and the fertile lands of the Ukraine. Their spearheads were still being harassed by largely unescorted formations of Red Air Force bombers, however, and it remained the job of the Luftwaffe's *Jagdgruppen* to protect their ground comrades against such attack.

During these operations another 20 or more pilots would achieve the kill, or kills, that put them on the first rung of the ladder to becoming Russian front semi-centurions.

Seven of them came from the ranks of Hannes Trautloft's JG 54 on the northern sector, although only one was a true tyro with no pre-*Barbarossa* kills to his name. This was I./JG 54's Unteroffizier Herbert Broennle,

Unteroffizier Gerhard Köppen's first two victories, however, were a brace of Ilyushin DB-3 bombers shot out of a formation attacking Constanza on 24 June. He is pictured here as a leutnant wearing the Oak Leaves awarded to him on 27 February 1942 for his then total of 72. This figure had risen to 85 by the time Köppen was forced to ditch in the Sea of Azov just over two months later

After being awarded the Knight's Cross for his 57 Russian front victories with JG 54, Leutnant Herbert Broennle was posted to JG 53 in the Mediterranean, where he served as acting-*Kapitän* of 2. Staffel. His sole success with his new unit was a B-24 claimed on 2 July 1943. Broennle was himself shot down by Spitfires over Sicily 48 hours later

Future semi-centurions Oberleutnants Heinz Lange (in shirt-sleeve order, left) and Hans Götz (centre) enjoy a well-earned break between missions

Heinz Kemethmüller is seen here wearing the Knight's Cross he won as a feldwebel with JG 3 in the USSR for his then total of 59 Russian front kills. After claiming just one more Soviet victim, he would be posted to JG 26. As a member of that *Geschwader's* 7. *Staffel*, Kemethmüller returned to Russia for two months in mid-1943, during which time he added another ten Red Air Force machines to his tally. Despite being wounded seven times, Oberleutnant Kemethmüller survived the war

who was credited with one of the 14 SB-2s downed by the *Gruppe* on 23 June.

On the same date Oberleutnant Wolfgang Späte of II./JG 54, whose only success so far had been a Yugoslav Blenheim downed during the brief campaign in the Balkans, also opened his Russian front score sheet with a pair of SB-2s destroyed within seconds of each other. Späte would later gain fame flying the Me 163 'Komet' rocket fighter, not only as leader of the test unit charged with developing this revolutionary (and highly unstable!) machine, but also as *Kommodore* of JG 400, the only *Geschwader* to fly it operationally.

Two of III./JG 54's pilots, both with previous victories to their credit, likewise claimed their first Soviet victories – yet more SB-2s – on 23 June. Unteroffizier Karl Kempf brought down one of the enemy bombers (his sixth kill overall), while Leutnant Max-Hellmuth Ostermann got a pair to take his tally to 11.

Forty-eight hours later, Leutnant Hans Götz of I./JG 54 also achieved a double, when he destroyed two Soviet 'I-18' fighters to add to his three earlier Battle of Britain victories. And on the last day of the month, III./JG 54's Oberleutnant Heinz Lange claimed a brace of DB-3s over southern Latvia (out of a total of 27 Soviet bombers credited to the *Gruppe* on 30 June). His only previous success dated back even further than Götz's trio of RAF fighters – a reconnaissance Blenheim intercepted and destroyed during the opening weeks of the Phoney War in the west.

The two *Jagdgeschwader* covering Army Group South's advance into the Ukraine were to produce eight fledgling 50+ *Experten* towards the end of June 1941. Two of them, both members of JG 3, achieved their first kills during this period, II./JG 3's Leutnant Ludwig Häfner identifying his victim, brought down east of the *Gruppe's* base at Hostynne on 24 June, as a 'Potez 63'. Unless he had shot down a Potez of the Rumanian Air Force by mistake, it is impossible to say exactly what type of machine had provided Häfner with his first victory!

Two more 'Potez 63s' were to be claimed by the *Gruppe* the following day. This would seem to rule out the 'shot down in error' scenario. The

most likely candidate would thus appear to be the Soviet Petlyakov Pe-2, a twin-engined, twin-tailed type not dissimilar to the French Potez and perhaps as yet unfamiliar to the pilots of II./JG 3, but one that they would first report encountering just three days later on 28 June.

Some confusion also surrounds the first kill claimed by Unteroffizier Heinz Kemethmüller of III./JG 3 on 29 June, which he described as a ZBK-19. This was the designation given to an experimental water-cooled engined development of the Polikarpov I-16 *Rata* built in the mid-1930s that failed to go into production. Despite (or perhaps because of) this, the normally obsessively secretive Soviets released details of the machine. It featured widely in the pre-war aviation press, and was even exhibited at the 1936 Paris Air Salon. But the aircraft claimed by Kemethmüller five years later was almost certainly the superficially similar MiG-3.

Of the other three pilots of JG 3 to claim their first Russian victims at this time, II. *Gruppe's* Feldwebel Walter Ohlrogge downed an I-16 on 25 June to add to his one previous success in the west. And while Feldwebel Georg Schentke of III./JG 3 had been credited with an I-16 (his fifth kill of the war) on 24 June, a day later Oberfeldwebel Eberhard von Boremski – also of 9. *Staffel* – would take his overall total to six with another pair of 'Potez 63's. True, the Red Air Force was still a new and largely unknown opponent, but III./JG 3's aircraft recognition seems to have been particularly hazy. Before the month

Given III./JG 3's somewhat dubious powers of aircraft recognition during the opening stages of *Barbarossa*, it would be interesting to speculate what this victorious pilot – returning to base southwest of Zhitomir, wings waggling to indicate a kill – is going to claim. In fact, on the date this photograph was taken, the *Gruppe* contented itself with a quartet of DB-3 bombers and a dozen assorted Polikarpov fighters

Leutnant Friedrich Geisshardt, the *Gruppen-Adjutant* of I.(J)/LG 2, was still waiting for his Knight's Cross when this photograph was taken in late June 1941. Note the unit's newly introduced, but now decidedly anachronistic, badge below the windscreen – an elaborate capital 'L' (for *Lehrgeschwader*) enclosing a map of Great Britain, with London prominently marked

'Toni' Lindner served with JG 51 'Mölders' throughout almost the entire war. He is pictured here sporting the Knight's Cross he received on 8 April 1944 for 62 victories – just 11 short of his final overall total

An early Russian front semi-centurion, Oberfeldwebel Heinrich Hoffmann (second from left) already had 60+ victories to his credit when this photograph was taken at IV./JG 51's Zhatalovka-East base in mid-September 1941. Next to him (in the forage cap) is Oberfähnrich Ernst Weismann, whose final tally of 69 Soviet kills was to earn him a posthumous Knight's Cross on 21 August 1942

was out, the *Gruppe* would also have added a quartet of Polish PZL P.37 *Los* bombers to their collective scoreboard!

Also on the southern sector, three more future semi-centurions opened their accounts against the Soviets with multiple kills to add to their existing totals. III./JG 77's Leutnant Emil Omert claimed a trio of SB-2s on 24 June to take his tally to five. Forty-eight hours later, the *Gruppen-Adjutant*, Oberleutnant Diethelm von Eichel-Streiber, went one better by downing four DB-3s in as many minutes, which also raised his overall score to five.

Another *Gruppen-Adjutant*, Leutnant Friedrich Geisshardt of I.(J)/LG 2, had been credited with an SB-2 bomber and a MiG-3 fighter on the second day of the campaign. This upped his total to date to exactly 20. A year earlier this figure would automatically have qualified him for the Knight's Cross, but such were the numbers of enemy aircraft now being shot down on the Russian front that this yardstick had already gone by the board. Geisshardt would have to wait two more months – and add six more Red Air Force machines to his score – before receiving the coveted award.

Not surprisingly, the heavy fighting that was taking place on the central sector as June 1941 drew to a close also produced a crop of new additions to the list of the Russian front's future 50+ *Experten*.

After its successes on the opening day of *Barbarossa*, I./JG 51 was credited with just one kill on 23 June. But the reconnaissance biplane brought down by 2. *Staffel's* Feldwebel Anton Lindner put him on the first rung of the ladder to becoming a semi-centurion. A week later, on 30 June, I./JG 51 was back in the thick of the action. The *Gruppe's* combined score on that date was 36. A third of that number were claimed by pilots who already had one or more Soviet machines under their belt – Bär, Bareuther, Höfemeier and Krafft – but the brace of SB-2s downed by Leutnant Erwin Fleig (taking his overall total to 11) were his first victories against the Red Air Force.

By coincidence, III./JG 51's collective score on 24 June, made up predominantly of SB-2s, had also been 36. And a third of that number fell to just two pilots. Oberleutnant Karl-Heinz Schnell, *Staffelkapitän* of 9./JG 51, upped his pre-*Barbarossa* tally of nine to 16 by claiming seven enemy bombers in three separate missions during the course of the day.

Perhaps even more impressive was the performance of one of Schnell's 9. *Staffel* pilots, Oberfeldwebel Edmund Wagner, who made his scoring debut with five kills in the same three engagements.

Like I. *Gruppe*, IV./JG 51 had an almost barren day on 23 June. The Red Air Force was conspicuous by its absence in its sector, and most of the daylight hours were spent ground-strafing Soviet troop columns and artillery emplacements. The sole aerial success of the day was a single SB-2 snooper

caught and despatched by 12. *Staffel's* Feldwebel Heinrich Hoffmann in mid-evening – his second kill of the war and first in the east. Five days later, on 28 June, another member of 12./JG 51, Feldwebel Herbert Friebel, would open his score sheet with an Ilyushin DB-3 south-west of Bobruisk.

IV./JG 51 was still operating alongside I./JG 53, and the latter *Gruppe* produced just one future 50+ *Experte* during this early-invasion period – Leutnant Wolfgang Tonne, whose pair of Tupolev SB-2 bombers claimed on 24 June (his first Russian front victories) raised his current total to seven.

Thus, by the end of the first nine days of Operation *Barbarossa*, some 57 pilots had already achieved the first victory, or victories, that would set them on the path to becoming Russian front semi-centurions. In the weeks, months and years ahead, nearly 100 others would follow them. But the longer the war against the Soviet Union lasted, the more difficult the conditions facing these later arrivals became.

'The happy time', as some early veterans of the air war in the east referred to the summer of 1941 – a time of large, untidy phalanxes of unescorted, mainly obsolescent bombers almost lining up to be slaughtered – could not go on for ever. In fact, even before summer had given way to early autumn, the Red Air Force had rebuilt the strength of its frontal fighter defences. The *Jagdgruppen's* daily score sheets reflected this gradual, but irreversible, change, with collective claims for a dozen or more bombers at a time, which had previously been the norm, now being replaced by appreciably fewer victories, most of them fighters.

Admittedly, these fighters were not the most modern of types either. But they sufficed to blunt the German advance until the onset of winter brought a virtual halt to the campaign of 1941. By then another 35 Luftwaffe pilots would have joined the ranks of the future semi-centurions. Also by that time six of those who had been engaged in *Barbarossa* from the very beginning would actually have topped the 50 mark . . . but two of the six were already dead.

Representative of the fighter opposition faced by the *Jagdgruppen* during the opening phases of *Barbarossa* were these captured Polikarpov fighters – an I-153 biplane in the foreground and an I-16 monoplane just visible in the background

ALL ROADS LEAD EAST

Among the earliest of the higher decorations awarded to Russian front fighter pilots were the Oak Leaves presented to Hauptmann Herbert Ihlefeld, *Gruppenkommandeur* of I.(J)/LG 2, and Major Günther Lützow, *Geschwaderkommodore* of JG 3. These were conferred on 27 June and 20 July for 40 and 42 victories respectively. Both pilots were already wearing the Knight's Cross for earlier successes in the west prior to *Barbarossa*, and the totals that won them the Oak Leaves were still in line with the original criteria laid down for this prestigious award. Werner Mölders and Adolf Galland had been the first two pilots to receive the Oak Leaves back in September 1940 after each had attained his 40th victory.

But with the huge numbers of Soviet aircraft being shot down during the opening rounds of the war in the east, there was now a very real danger of the Knight's Cross itself becoming devalued. The initial benchmark figure that would assure a Luftwaffe fighter pilot of his winning the Knight's Cross had been 20 enemy aircraft destroyed. Against western opponents this had represented a considerable achievement, usually gained only after weeks, if not months, of hard campaigning. But on the Russian front some pilots had been bringing down four or five machines of the Red Air Force in a single day.

The RLM (Reich's Air Ministry) came up with the obvious answer – increase the number of victories required to win the award. The figure set would continue to escalate, sometimes without apparent rhyme or reason, throughout the remainder of the war against the Soviet Union. Towards its end, the scores amassed by some Luftwaffe fighter pilots would be well into treble figures before the Knight's Cross was hung around their necks (see *Aircraft of the Aces 37*).

The effect of these changes was felt right from the start, however. When the first two future semi-centurions to be awarded the Knight's Cross – Heinz Bär and Richard Leppla, both of JG 51 – received their decorations in July 1941, each had already been credited with seven victories over and above the previously obligatory 20. And the scores of five of August's six recipients ranged between 26 and 32, with the sixth having achieved 40! It is

An *Experte* in the making. The rudder of this *Friedrich* ('Black 5' of 8./JG 54's Oberleutnant Heinz Lange) records its pilot's victories to date – a single western kill (an RAF Blenheim on 30 October 1939) and four Soviet DB-3s. This photograph was taken at Dünaburg, in Latvia, on 5 July 1941

perhaps worth recording that the 40 had been racked up by the only NCO pilot among the six, Oberfeldwebel Heinrich Hoffmann, who was a member of 'Pritzl' Bär's 12./JG 51.

A smiling Hauptmann Richard Leppla, *Gruppenkommandeur* of III./JG 51, wearing the Knight's Cross that resulted from his 27th victory, a DB-3 downed on 26 July 1941 . . .

Another result of the increase in the number of kills needed to win the Knight's Cross was that it widened still further the already yawning gap between it and the much lowlier Iron Cross, First Class. The latter was presented for an individual act, or acts, of bravery, whereas the Knight's Cross was originally instituted to honour a deed, or conduct, of a 'battle-decisive' nature. And there was nothing to bridge the chasm that existed between the two.

The lack of any such 'intermediate decoration' had been exercising the minds of those in authority long before the launch of *Barbarossa*. Suggestions were put forward for a Golden Iron Cross, or an Iron Cross with Oak Leaf Cluster. But the final arbiter in the matter, the *Führer* himself, rejected both these ideas. Instead, on 12 September 1941, he authorised the introduction of an entirely new award – the German Cross in Gold.

The only Wehrmacht (German armed forces) decoration for bravery to be worn on the *right* breast, the German Cross in Gold was a somewhat oversized and ornate affair. It consisted of a large swastika encircled by a golden laurel wreath, the whole backed by a starburst of dark-grey metal, edged in silver. Because of its weight and size, many recipients, particularly among the ground troops, would find it an encumbrance and

. . . while it was No 31 – yet another DB-3, this one downed on 28 July – that won his fellow *Gruppenkommandeur* Hauptmann Karl-Gottfried Nordmann of IV./JG 51 (whose *Friedrich* is pictured here) his Knight's Cross on 1 August 1941

refuse to wear it in battle. A cloth version was subsequently produced with only the laurel wreath in metal.

And with typical irreverence, Luftwaffe fighter pilots soon had their own nicknames for the award. Because the central swastika motif in its gold surround greatly resembled the much smaller badges proudly sported by the early members of the Nazi party, some referred to it as the 'Party badge for the short-sighted'. Others, in keeping with the culinary theme that had seen the Oak Leaves christened the 'Cauliflower' and the Swords dubbed the 'Knife and fork', would simply call it the 'Fried egg'!

The steadily rising scores of the Russian front *Jagdflieger* led to the introduction of the intermediate German Cross in Gold, as modelled here by Leutnant Hans Fuss, the *Staffelkapitän* of 6./JG 3, in the summer of 1942. Fuss received the award on 10 July 1942, and it was to be followed by the Knight's Cross – for his then total of 60 Soviet aircraft destroyed – on 23 August

The first future 50+ ace of the Russian front to be awarded the German Cross in Gold was Hauptmann Reinhard Seiler, the recently appointed *Gruppenkommandeur* of III./JG 54. He received the decoration on 15 October 1941, having claimed his 35th kill – an I-15 downed near Leningrad – just four days earlier. Seven more victories would then earn 'Seppl' Seiler the Knight's Cross on 20 December.

The next three German Crosses were all presented on 24 September. They went to Oberfeldwebel Karl Kempf of Seiler's III./JG 54, the 19-year-old Leutnant Horst Hannig of II./JG 54, and Feldwebel Otto Tange of II./JG 51. All three currently had totals of 30+, and all three would also be sporting the Knight's Cross by the spring of 1942.

Although the German Cross in Gold fell between the Iron Cross, First Class, and the Knight's Cross in order of importance, its award was not a prerequisite for winning the higher decoration. In other words, a pilot did not *have* to have the German Cross before he could be considered for the Knight's Cross. Some Knight's Cross winners never did receive the German Cross in Gold. Others were awarded the two decorations in seemingly reverse order. All three of the next trio of Russian front pilots to be given the German Cross in Gold, for example – Hauptmann Richard Leppla and Oberleutnants Wolfgang Späte and Kurt Ubben – were already wearing the Knight's Cross.

The flurry of awards conferred during the late summer and early autumn of 1941 were indicative of the rapidly rising personal tallies of many of the fighter pilots engaged on the Russian front. Most of these early participants in *Barbarossa* were adding to score sheets already opened against the western allies. One such was Leutnant Heinz Bär of 1./JG 51, who had embarked upon the campaign in the east with a total standing at 17.

Since promoted to oberleutnant and appointed *Staffelkapitän* of 12./JG 51, Bär's 67th victory – one of a pair of Petlyakov Pe-2s claimed on the evening of 9 August 1941 – was thus the 50th Red Air Force machine he had brought down. Bär was the first of the semi-centurions to reach this figure.

The first Russian front semi-centurion to receive the German Cross in Gold had been Hauptmann Reinhard Seiler on 15 October 1941. He too was awarded the Knight's Cross shortly afterwards – on 20 December – for a total of 42. Perversely, however, although the latter can just be made out around his neck, there is no sign of the 'Fried egg' on that decidedly non-regulation leather jacket (although the Iron Cross is prominently displayed on his left breast). On the original print of this photograph two stitches are visible below the pocket zipper on the right – was 'Seppl' Seiler perhaps one of those who decided that Hitler's new decoration was too bulky to be worn in action?

Three more pilots got to their Russian front half-centuries in September. Two were Günther Lützow and Karl-Gottfried Nordmann (with their 68th and 59th kills respectively). The third was Oberfeldwebel Heinrich Hoffmann, the NCO pilot of Bär's *Staffel* who had amassed 40 kills before being awarded his Knight's Cross. As Hoffmann had only one pre-*Barbarossa* success to his credit – a Spitfire downed during the Battle of Britain – it was his 51st victory (the first of three Red Air Force machines credited to him on 4 September) that elevated him to the ranks of the semi-centurions. It was a position he would enjoy for less than a month before achieving the unhappy distinction of being the first of their number to be killed in action.

It was on 3 October 1941, moments after claiming his 63rd kill, that Hoffmann's 'Brown 2' was brought down while attacking Ilyushin Il-2 *Shturmoviks* south of Yelnya. His loss was keenly felt, not just by his fellow members of 12. *Staffel*, but by the entire *Geschwader*, for at the time of his death the now little known Hoffmann was the fourth highest scorer yet produced by JG 51. Only Werner Mölders (101 victories, and since banned from operational flying), Heinz Bär (80 victories, and currently recovering in hospital after crash-landing behind enemy lines) and Hermann-Friedrich Joppien (70 victories, 28 of them in the east before being killed in action on 25 August) having scored more.

In recognition of his achievements, Oberfeldwebel Heinrich Hoffmann was the first fighter pilot of non-commissioned rank to be honoured with posthumous Oak Leaves.

The career of one of October's two newly fledged semi-centurions – another oberfeldwebel of JG 51 – was to be even briefer than Hoffmann's. All of Edmund Wagner's victories were scored on the Russian front. The first five, all bombers, he had claimed on 24 June. His 50th, an 'I-61' fighter, was despatched on 28 October. He added another five to his tally in the ensuing fortnight before he was himself shot down and killed in action against a formation of Pe-2 bombers on 13 November. His final total of 55 had not sufficed for a German Cross in Gold, but Oberfeldwebel Edmund Wagner of 9./JG 51 was also honoured posthumously with a Knight's Cross four days after his death.

As the winter of 1941 tightened its grip on the battlefields, Army Group North was at the gates of Leningrad and Army Group South was occupying almost the whole of the Ukraine. But the great prize in the centre – Moscow – remained untaken. And when German ground forces

An unusually serious Oberfeldwebel Heinrich Hoffmann of 12./JG 51. He was the first Russian front semi-centurion to be killed in action

A pair of *Friedrichs* from III./JG 51 pictured on the central sector in the autumn of 1941

Winter 1941-42 on the northern sector. As two Bf 109Fs of II./JG 54 (foreground) are readied for their next mission, a *Staffel* of Ju 87D Stukas takes off for another strike somewhere along the Leningrad/Volkhov front

resumed their offensives in the spring of 1942, Hitler's gaze was no longer focused on the capital city of the Soviet Union. His attention had turned instead to the south, and the enemy's rich oilfields down in the Caucasus region. Much of the major action of the second year of the war in the east was thus to take place on the southern sector.

Meanwhile, in the north, the siege of Leningrad would continue, and on the central sector, once the Red Army's winter counter-offensive had run its course, the front stabilised into little more than a holding war.

The enforced lack of aerial activity during the depths of the winter is indicated by the fact that, in the first two months of 1942, only three pilots – Bernd Gallowitsch, Karl Kempf and Leopold Steinbatz – all with scores in the low 40s, were awarded the Knight's Cross as they edged their way towards the half-century.

One who did top the 50 mark during this period, however, was III./JG 52's Feldwebel Gerhard Köppen. He had received the Knight's Cross on 18 December 1941 for his then 40 victories. Over the following weeks he had continued to add steadily to this number. The four machines of the Red Air Force that he downed on 24 February 1942

23

Seen here in September 1941 as the *Staffelkapitän* of 6./JG 54, being congratulated upon winning the Knight's Cross, Hauptmann Franz Eckerle (right) had been appointed *Gruppenkommandeur* of II./JG 54 by the time he was reported missing on 14 February 1942 – the third Russian front semi-centurion casualty

took his tally – all scored on the Russian front – to 72, and earned him the Oak Leaves three days later.

The indestructible Heinz Bär was also back in action at the head of his 12./JG 51 by this time. He had been awarded the Swords on 16 February for his overall total of 90 enemy aircraft destroyed. Less fortunate was Hauptmann Franz Eckerle, the *Gruppenkommandeur* of I./JG 54. Like Bär earlier, he too had been forced to make an emergency landing behind enemy lines (southeast of Schlüsselburg on 14 February 1942). But unlike Bär he was unable to make his way back to friendly territory and was posted missing, presumed killed.

A well-known aerobatic pilot before the war, Eckerle had been one of September 1941's seven Knight's Cross recipients (for a score of 30, all but four in the east). He was the third Russian front semi-centurion to be lost. His final overall total of 59 resulted in another set of posthumous Oak Leaves, awarded on 12 March 1942.

The resumption of operations come the spring thaw of March 1942 is also reflected in the number of decorations awarded that month. Five of the six Knight's Crosses to be conferred again went to pilots who had reached, or topped, the 40 mark, but had yet to attain their half-century. The sixth had done so, but his achievements had gone unrecognised. The pilot in question, Leutnant Hans Strelow, *Staffelkapitän* of 5./JG 51, did not disguise his feelings about this apparent oversight. The rudder of his *Friedrich*, with all his victories carefully recorded on it, also bore the drawing of a Knight's Cross followed by a large question mark!

By the time Hans Strelow received the Knight's Cross he so clearly felt entitled to – on 18 March

The rudder of Leutnant Hans Strelow's *Friedrich* makes his feelings perfectly clear – 'I've got the 40 kills, when do I get my Knight's Cross?'

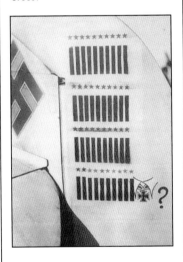

Appointed *Gruppenkommandeur* of III./JG 77 on 5 September 1941, just 24 hours after winning his Knight's Cross, it took Hauptmann Kurt Ubben an additional six months and 40 kills before he was recommended for the Oak Leaves . . .

... which he received from the hands of the *Führer* in person. He is seen here in the centre of the line-up, flanked by two members of JG 54. In the foreground (right) is Oberleutnant Max-Hellmuth Ostermann, who is just being presented with his Oak Leaves by Hitler, while, half-hidden in shadow at the far end, future 177-victory Russian front *Experte* Hauptmann Hans Philipp waits to receive the Swords for his current total of 82 (for details of Philipp's career see *Osprey Aircraft of the Aces 37*)

– his total was standing at 52. He more than made his point by adding another 14 kills over the course of the next six days. And the authorities more than made amends by promptly awarding him the Oak Leaves. The 20-year-old Berliner thereby became the youngest wearer of the Oak Leaves in the war to date.

Two older hands, Oberleutnant Max-Hellmuth Ostermann of JG 54 and JG 77's Kurt Ubben, also got their Oak Leaves in March 1942 – for totals of 62 and 69 respectively. They were followed in April by Wolfgang Späte (72 victories, all but one on the Russian front), and in May Oberleutnant Ostermann was awarded the Swords for reaching his century (91 in the east).

The number of semi-centurions was beginning to climb, but so too were their losses. They suffered three casualties in May 1942 alone, two of them recent Oak Leaves winners.

On 5 May Gerhard Köppen of III./JG 52 was forced to ditch in the Sea of Azov when his engine was hit during an engagement with Pe-2s. A fellow pilot who had seen him climb out of his machine continued to circle overhead until his fuel ran low. Although a pair of fighters from neighbouring JG 77 were immediately despatched to the scene, they saw no sign of Köppen in the water – just a pair of Soviet MTBs heading back to the safety of the coast. Whether Gerhard Köppen drowned or became a prisoner of the Russians remains uncertain to this day.

The latter fate was one that the young Hans Strelow was determined to avoid at all costs. He too was forced down behind enemy lines after a running fight with a formation of Pe-2s near Mtsensk on the central sector on 22 May. Rather than be captured by the Red Army, it is reported that the *Kapitän* of 5./JG 51 shot himself. The Petlyakov he had just claimed took his Russian front total to 68.

The highest scoring semi-centurion of them all was Oberfeldwebel Leopold 'Bazi' Steinbatz of 9./JG 52, whose total stood at 99 when he was shot down by Soviet flak on 15 June 1942. He is pictured here wearing the Oak Leaves he had won just 13 days earlier. Steinbatz would become the first NCO of the entire Wehrmacht ever to receive the Swords – albeit posthumously – which were announced on 23 June 1942

Exactly a week after Strelow's loss, another of JG 51's semi-centurions came down over enemy territory. Leutnant Erwin Fleig had been with the *Geschwader* since mid-1940. Not only had he often flown as Werner Mölders' wingman, the two had become close personal friends, and Erwin Fleig had been a witness at the *Kommodore's* wedding in September 1941. After baling out of his damaged *Friedrich* near Podorye on 29 May, Fleig was to spend many years in Soviet captivity, not being returned to Germany until long after the war.

June 1942 saw two more pilots awarded the Oak Leaves. Oberfeldwebel Leopold Steinbatz of 9./JG 52 had claimed his first kill (an I-16 southeast of Kiev) on 4 August 1941. In February 1942 he had received the Knight's Cross for a total of 42. By the beginning of June he had all but doubled that score to 83, claiming 35 kills in May alone.

On 15 June, less than a fortnight after being presented with the Oak Leaves, 'Bazi' Steinbatz was brought down by Soviet anti-aircraft fire. By then his score had risen to just one short of a century, making him the 11th ranking Luftwaffe fighter pilot at that time. He also became the first ever NCO in the entire Wehrmacht to be awarded the Swords when he was honoured posthumously on 23 June.

It was on that same 23 June that I.(J)/LG 2's Oberleutnant Friedrich Geisshardt received his Oak Leaves for an overall total of 79 victories.

Between April and June 1942, nine pilots won the Knight's Cross. Their scores ranged from 40 to 49. They were all nudging the 50 barrier, but none had yet broken through it. All that was to change in August when the RLM clearly upped the award criteria by another notch. That month's four Knight's Cross recipients all had totals well in excess of 50. Thereafter, it became very rare for a pilot with a score below that figure to be awarded the Knight's Cross (there are believed to have been only five). In effect, the conferral of a Knight's Cross would henceforth almost guarantee the recipient's being, or soon becoming, a semi-centurion.

August 1942 was a turning point in another way too. It was the first month in which new additions to the ranks of the semi-centurions were outnumbered by their losses. Two of the four Knight's Crosses awarded were posthumous, and the remaining pair went to pilots with only weeks to live.

Two shots that illustrate the Luftwaffe's continuing supremacy 12 months into the air war on the Russian front – the tail of an Il-2 shot down by future semi-centurion Oberfeldwebel Otto Wessling of 9./JG 3 on 11 June 1942 . . .

... and the rudder of the Swords-wearing Hauptmann Heinz Bär – now *Gruppenkommandeur* of I./JG 77 on the Crimea – displaying his current total of 113 kills, the last two a brace of I-16s downed over the Kerch Straits on 27 June 1942

But in the latter half of 1942 things suddenly changed and losses started to climb. In August alone, five semi-centurions were killed or reported missing. One of them was 53-victory Karl Sattig, *Staffelkapitän* of 6./JG 54, who went down in the Rzhev area on 10 August ...

The latter were Hauptmann Joachim Wandel and Leutnant Hans Fuss, the *Staffelkapitäne* of 5./JG 54 and 6./JG 3 respectively. Wandel received his Knight's Cross on 21 August for a total of 64 victories. He would add 11 more before being killed on 7 October when his *Gustav* dived vertically into the ground during a low-level dogfight with LaGG-3s northeast of Oshtashkov.

Hans Fuss was awarded the Knight's Cross on 23 August for his 60 kills. He too would claim 11 more Soviet victims before his Bf 109G-2 was badly damaged in a dogfight with a gaggle of Yak-1s on 14 September. Although he made it back to II./JG 3's base at Dedyurevo, north of Vyazma, the engine of Fuss' machine cut out as he attempted an emergency landing. It somersaulted several times and he suffered severe injuries, from which he died in a Berlin hospital on 10 November.

The first of the month's two posthumous Knight's Crosses was awarded to Oberleutnant Ernst Weismann of IV./JG 51. He had been forced to bale out of his stricken 'Brown 12' during a dogfight north of Rzhev on 13 August. His Knight's Cross was announced eight days later. All 69 of his victories had been claimed on the Russian front. The second award went to I./JG 52's Oberfeldwebel Heinz-Wilhelm Ahnert. He had reached his half-century on 9 July, and had since added a further seven kills to his score before being brought down by return fire from a Pe-2 near Koptevo on 23 August. His Knight's Cross was awarded posthumously that same day. Like Weismann, all of Ahnert's victories had been claimed over Russia.

Three other Russian front semi-centurions were lost in August. In fact on 12 May Oberleutnant Max-Hellmuth Ostermann, the *Staffelkapitän* of 8./JG 54, had been the sixth Luftwaffe fighter pilot to achieve 100 kills (for which he received the Swords), but the first nine of these had been claimed prior to *Barbarossa*. Unlike most pilots, who disliked venturing too far over Soviet-held territory for obvious reasons, Ostermann revelled in long-distance patrols deep into enemy airspace. But it was one such *freie Jagd* sweep that was to prove his undoing. Although an expert dogfighter, Ostermann met his match when he was intercepted and shot down by nine enemy fighters near Ammosovo on 9 August. His final Russian front total was 93.

The day after Ostermann's loss, fellow *Staffelkapitän* Hauptmann Karl Sattig of 6./JG 54 was reported missing in the Rzhev area. A reconnaissance pilot at the beginning of the war, Sattig had converted to fighters in 1941. All of his 53 kills had been scored in Russia, two of them by night. 4./JG 52's Leutnant Waldemar Semelka had also claimed all his 65 successes in the east, the first on the opening day of the campaign. On 21 August he too was reported missing. Both Sattig and Semelka would be honoured with posthumous Knight's Crosses the following month.

September 1942 was to see more decorations awarded to semi-centurions than any other month during the course of the war in the east. In addition to those of Sattig and Semelka mentioned above, ten other Knight's Crosses were conferred. Eight of the recipients had scores ranging between 50 and 65, but the remaining two fell some way outside what was presumably the then current 50-60 yardstick.

Leutnant Walter Zellot, the *Staffelkapitän* of 2./JG 53, was another who had claimed his first kill on the opening day of *Barbarossa*. Since that time he had amassed 77 more (including three during I./JG 53's brief initial deployment in the Mediterranean theatre), before finally being presented with the Knight's Cross on 3 September.

Fellow *Staffelkapitän* Oberleutnant Wolfgang Tonne of 3./JG 53 had five victories fewer than Zellot when he received his Knight's Cross three days later. But his total of 73 – all but five scored in Russia – was still way above the prevailing norm. The powers-that-be made up for their apparent tardiness in present-

. . . and three days later 12./JG 51's Oberleutnant Ernst Weismann was also lost near Rzhev. He is pictured here (centre) with the carved 'victory stick' on which he recorded all of his 69 kills. Both Sattig and Weismann would be honoured with posthumous Knight's Crosses (in September and August respectively)

ing Tonne with the Knight's Cross by promptly awarding him the Oak Leaves later that same month – on 24 September – for an overall total of 101. But Walter Zellot would not live to get the same treatment.

On 10 September, exactly one week after receiving the Knight's Cross, and with seven more kills added to his score in the interim, he was shot down by Soviet anti-aircraft fire during a low-level strafing attack.

One of September's two other semi-centurion casualties, both oberfeldwebels, had been a member of Zellot's 2./JG 53. Alfred Franke's score was standing at 59 when he was killed in action just 24 hours before his *Staffelkapitän*. His promotion to leutnant was posthumous, as was his Knight's Cross, announced on 29 October. By contrast, JG 52's Kurt Ratzlaff received no further official recognition after being shot down and taken prisoner on 29 September – 'all' that his final total of 68 Soviet aircraft destroyed had earned him had been the German Cross in Gold, awarded four months earlier.

During the late summer and early autumn, the ground forces on the southern sector had made considerable territorial gains. As the 1942 offensive progressed, Army Group South had been divided into Army Groups A and B. On the right, or southernmost, flank of the twin-pronged advance, Army Group A, in particular, had thrust deep down into the Caucasus – although the oilfields along the shores of the Caspian Sea still remained tantalisingly just out of reach.

Meanwhile, Army Group B on the left flank had crossed the River Don and was heading towards Stalingrad. Troops of the spearheading *6. Armee* reached the outskirts of the city late in August, but all attempts to take it would fail. As autumn gave way to an increasingly harsh winter, the Red Army's stubborn defence of its leader's namesake city on the west bank of the River Volga would result in the fiercest, bloodiest and undoubtedly most famous battle of the entire Russian front campaign. It ended in the complete annihilation of the encircled and starving *6. Armee*.

Stalingrad has since gone down in history as the major turning point of the war in the east. Thereafter, Hitler's ground forces would be almost constantly on the defensive. No less so the Luftwaffe. Semi-centurions Waldemar Semelka, Walter Zellot and Alfred Franke had all fallen in front of the city. They would not be the last.

STALINGRAD AND KURSK

Against a backdrop of the looming, but as yet unforeseen, catastrophe of Stalingrad, October 1942 was very much a repetition of the previous month. Eight more Knight's Crosses were awarded, all to pilots with scores of 50 or more. To offset this there were two further losses.

The first had been that of Hauptmann Joachim Wandel described in the previous chapter. October's other casualty was 2./JG 52's Oberfeldwebel Berthold Grassmuck. With one victory already to his name, he had claimed his first Russian victim (an I-16) on 5 October 1941, three days after I./JG 52's belated arrival on the Russian front. He reached his half-century on 6 August 1942 and, with a score of 56, had been one of September's ten Knight's Cross recipients.

Within hours of the award Grassmuck was on his way to Stalingrad's Pitomnik airfield with the rest of I./JG 52. There, he would take his overall total to 65 before being killed in action on 28 October when the engine of his fighter was hit by Soviet anti-aircraft fire and he came down just short of base. A *Gruppe* diarist recorded;

'On 28 October Knight's Cross holder Oberfeldwebel Grassmuck, unbeaten in the air by the enemy, crashed six kilometres east of the field and was laid to rest with full military honours in the heroes' cemetery at Pitomnik airfield.'

Grassmuck's comrades were credited with 116 Red Air Force machines shot down during their six-week stay at Pitomnik. Then, on 5 November, after handing their *Gustavs* over to the resident JG 3, they were withdrawn to Rostov-on-Don for rest and refit.

The three *Gruppen* of JG 3 had been supporting Army Group B during the summer as it advanced on Stalingrad. Most of their number had then been transferred forward to Pitomnik, only some 20 kilometres from the city's centre, in September. And it was they who would bear the brunt of the fighter war over and around the beleaguered *6. Armee* in the terrible weeks ahead.

At first this simply meant more of the same kind of missions that had successfully brought them as far as the Volga – missions to protect the ground troops from ever increasing enemy air attack, and *freie Jagd* fighter sweeps. It was one of the latter that cost the life of Leutnant Ludwig Häfner, the *Staffelkapitän* of 3./JG 3, who became yet another victim of the Red Army's murderous anti-aircraft fire. His 'Yellow 6' was brought down on 10 November while ground strafing a Soviet fighter airfield 80 kilometres to the east of Stalingrad. Moments before, Häfner had claimed one of the Yak-1s defending the field. It was his 52nd kill (his first had been another of those mysterious 'Potez 63s' downed in 1941), and would earn him a posthumous Knight's Cross on 24 December.

The first of October's two casualties. Hauptmann Joachim Wandel, *Staffelkapitän* of 5./JG 54, was lost during a dogfight with LaGG-3s on 7 October 1942 . . .

. . . and exactly three weeks after Wandel was killed on the northern sector, I./JG 52's Oberfeldwebel Berthold Grassmuck lost his life to Soviet flak as the fighting around Stalingrad intensified

The only semi-centurion lost while serving with the *Platzschutzstaffel Pitomnik* was 2./JG 3's Leutnant Georg Schentke, who baled out over enemy territory on Christmas Day 1942. He is seen here as an oberfeldwebel (centre) earlier in the year when a member of III./JG 3 with, left, *Gruppenkommandeur* Major Karl-Heinz Greisert (killed in action 22 July 1942) and fellow 9. *Staffel* oberfeldwebel, and semi-centurion, Walter Ohlrogge (seriously wounded on 5 September 1942 after claiming his 74th Soviet victim)

Just nine days after Häfner's loss, the Russians launched massive counter-offensives to the north and south of Stalingrad. On 22 November the jaws of the two pincers met near Kalach, on the River Don, and Stalingrad was cut off. As the Red Army closed in on the beleaguered city from all sides, conditions quickly deteriorated. Luftwaffe transport crews made superhuman efforts to make good *Reichsmarschall* Göring's foolhardy boast that he could keep the defenders supplied by air. It was an impossible task.

Lack of equipment and facilities, the appalling weather – blizzards in the air, deep snow on the ground – and, above all, the thousands of anti-aircraft guns encircling the city, and packed particularly densely in 'flak lanes' along the transports' routes of approach to Pitomnik, kept supplies down to a bare fraction of what was actually required to keep 6. *Armee* alive and fighting.

Stalingrad 1941-42. Troops unload supplies flown in to Pitomnik by Ju 52/3ms of *Blindflugschule* (Blind Flying School) 2. The transport crews made superhuman efforts to keep the beleaguered 6. *Armee* supplied by air . . .

... while the fighters did all they could to protect the vulnerable Junkers tri-motors ...

... but it was a hopeless task. After the loss of Pitomnik, supplies had to be air-dropped either by parachute, or in special containers such as that shown here. The purpose-built *Verpflegungsabwurfkiste* (Airdrop Supply Crate) 500, slung beneath the belly of a He 111 bomber, was fitted with a parachute at one end (right) and a buffer at the other to reduce the force of impact as it hit the ground

Within a week of Stalingrad's encirclement, the *Gustavs* of JG 3 were withdrawn to the complex of airfields around Morosovskaya behind the Don, one of the two main supply bases for flights into the city. But calls had gone out for volunteers to form a *Staffel* within the perimeter itself. Many answered the appeal – enough to man the unit on a rotational basis. Among those who served with the *Platzschutzstaffel Pitomnik* (Pitomnik Airfield Defence Squadron) were future semi-centurions Leutnant Gustav Frielinghaus and Feldwebel Hans Grünberg.

Their job was to protect the vulnerable transports from air attack on the last leg of the supply run into Pitomnik, and to cover them during their hurried turnarounds on the ground as they unloaded stores and took aboard the wounded waiting for evacuation. Only one 50+ *Experte* is believed to have been lost during the *Platzschutzstaffel's* brief existence. This was 2./JG 3's Leutnant Georg Schentke who, after claiming his 86th Russian front victim (probably an Il-2), was himself forced to bale out over enemy-held territory to the west of the shrinking Stalingrad perimeter.

Despite the Luftwaffe's valiant efforts, the *6. Armee* was slowly starving to death. By early January 1943 its daily rations were 200 grams of horsemeat (including bones), 75 grams – or two slices – of bread, 12 grams of fat, 11 grams of sugar and one cigarette per man. The pilots and groundcrews of the Pitomnik *Staffel* suffered the same hardships. One described what conditions were like towards the end;

'We were all physically exhausted. Most of our machines were damaged in one way or another, and could only be kept operational with immense difficulty due to almost constant enemy bombardment and attack from the air. We had to contend with freezing temperatures and an almost complete lack of supplies, spare parts and equipment. Even after the engines had been warmed up, our machines could only be started by vigorous cranking. But the mechanics could usually make only one or two turns of the handle before collapsing from cold and hunger.

'And all the while the field was under near continual air attack by day and by night. Time and again our machines suffered fresh damage from shrapnel and bomb splinters because, despite the cold, they were parked completely unprotected out in the open at the end of the take-off strip.'

In mid-January the pilots were ordered to fly out of Pitomnik and rejoin their *Gruppen*, which by now were some 350 kilometres away to the west behind the River Donets. Many of the mechanics and groundcrews were not so fortunate. At least 30 of them accompanied the survivors of *6. Armee* into Soviet captivity when *Generalfeldmarschall* Friedrich von Paulus finally surrendered on 2 February 1943.

Although German attention had been focused on the unfolding tragedy of Stalingrad, air operations had been continuing unabated on the other fronts. The last two months of 1942 had seen eight new Knight's Crosses awarded, but also two more losses among the growing ranks of the semi-centurions.

On 9 November 8./JG 54's Leutnant Hans-Joachim Heyer had collided with a Soviet fighter during a dogfight near Gorodok, on the Leningrad front. Only one parachute was observed as the two machines plunged to earth behind enemy lines. Whether it was Heyer or his opponent who managed to extricate himself is not known. But Heyer was posted missing. His final Russian front total of 53 (including three by night) earned him a posthumous Knight's Cross on 25 November.

Hauptmann Heinrich Krafft, the *Gruppenkommandeur* of I./JG 51, was already wearing the Knight's Cross when he was brought down by Soviet flak on the central sector on 14 December. 'Gaudi' Krafft was the first of the 50+ *Experten* (his exact total of Russian front victories was 74) to be lost while flying a Focke-Wulf Fw 190. This presents an added complication to any survey, such as the present work, that attempts to detail the exploits of those pilots who exceeded the half-century while flying the Bf 109 in the war against the Soviet Union.

Several *Jagdgeschwader*, most notably JGs 5, 51 and 54, converted from the Bf 109 onto the Fw 190 during the course of the campaign (with the bulk of JG 51 subsequently reverting to Messerschmitts again). It is therefore not always possible to tell with absolute certainty what type a pilot was flying when he claimed a particular victory. Although most *Jagdgruppen* were withdrawn from the front to carry out re-equipment and then returned to operations on their new mounts, some units converted in the field and, for a brief period at least, flew both Bf 109s and Fw 190s at the same time.

The rule of thumb thus adopted here is that if a pilot is known to have belonged to a specific unit prior to its conversion onto the Fw 190, he is assumed to have achieved at least some – if not the majority – of his 50+ victories on Bf 109s and is therefore included in these pages (see also appendix). If, however, it is on record that he joined the unit upon, or after, its final re-equipment with Focke-Wulfs, then he is not (the reader is referred to *Osprey Aircraft of the Aces 6 - Focke-Wulf Fw 190 Aces of the Russian Front* for further details).

The first Russian front semi-centurion casualty of 1943 represented another first – the first to be lost in a different theatre of war. Leutnant

Photographed on 4 November 1942 clutching a bouquet of flowers, a bottle of advocaat and a certificate confirming his having just achieved JG 54's 3000th collective victory of the war to date, Leutnant Hans-Joachim Heyer was lost in a mid-air collision with a Soviet fighter on the Leningrad front just five days later

A 96-victory Russian front *Experte*, Hauptmann Wolfgang Tonne, *Staffelkapitän* of 3./JG 53, was killed in a landing accident after his unit's transfer to Tunisia in November 1942

Johann Badum of 6./JG 77 had also been one of October 1942's nine Knight's Cross recipients for his 51 Soviet aircraft destroyed. Shortly thereafter JG 77 was ordered to North Africa to relieve the long-serving JG 27. Badum's II. *Gruppe* arrived in Libya early in December 1942. He would add a trio of P-40s to his Russian front total before himself being shot down by US fighters west of Tripoli on 12 January 1943.

In fact, very nearly half of all Russian front semi-centurions to be killed or reported missing between January 1943 and the end of the war would be lost in other theatres. Even after the defeat at Stalingrad, the campaign in the east was deemed too distant to prove an immediate threat to the Homeland. Those in power in Berlin perceived the growing strength of the air forces of the western allies in the United Kingdom and the Mediterranean as posing a far greater danger.

Over coming months Hitler would shamelessly bleed the Russian front units, at times almost to extinction, to prop up his shaky and inadequate defences in the south, the west and – above all – over the Reich itself.

After the loss of Stalingrad, German troops were forced constantly to give ground in the face of further large-scale Red Army offensives. This had all the makings of an even greater catastrophe. Army Group A was still fighting down in the Caucasus. If its forces could not get back across the Don, or reach the Crimea before the Russians started to advance westwards through the Ukraine, there was a very real risk of the entire army group being cut off and annihilated.

The southern sector was still the undisputed domain of JG 52. In terms of enemy aircraft destroyed, this was the most successful of all the *Jagdgeschwader* to see action against the Soviets. But its losses were commensurate. All three semi-centurions lost in the east early in 1943 came from its ranks. The first was Oberleutnant Gustav Denk, who had only just replaced the veteran 50+ *Experte* Hauptmann Rudolf 'Rudi' Resch as *Staffelkapitän* of 6./JG 52. Denk was killed near Krasnodar, in the Caucasus, on 13 February. His fledgling wingman recorded what happened;

'Our mission was to carry out a general reconnaissance of the front, with particular attention being paid to enemy airfields, and the types and numbers of machines in occupation.

'On the other side of the front all remained quiet. Not even a sign of flak to disturb us. But the cloud base, which had been at 3000 metres when we set out, gradually sank lower and lower. The mountains of the Caucasus had completely disappeared in cloud.

'My leader flew deeper into the flat Russian hinterland. There, the clouds were down to 400 metres. We were flying immediately below them. Suddenly, we spotted a Russian landing strip straight ahead of us. As we circled it, I saw a number of light courier aircraft dispersed around its edges. I was filled with the fever of the chase. Just as I was about to request permission to dive down and have a go at them, I heard over the R/T, "We'll carry out a low-level attack. Stick close to me and open fire when I do".

'Oberleutnant Denk tipped his machine onto one wing and dived at one of the parked crates. I waited a split-second and then followed him down, aiming at the same target. As I got nearer, however, I could see that it was already on fire, so I tried to line my sights up on the next one.

Like so many others, 1./JG 52's
Oberfeldwebel Karl Hammerl
disappeared without trace after
forced-landing behind enemy lines

Posing proudly some time in 1942,
and holding some kind of –
unfortunately unidentifiable – unit
trophy, Feldwebel Willi Nemitz of
5./JG 52 was one of the Luftwaffe's
oldest operational fighter pilots.
Appointed *Staffelkapitän* of
6./JG 52 on 1 March 1943, the now
Oberfeldwebel Nemitz was awarded
the Knight's Cross ten days later.
He wore the decoration for exactly
one month . . .

I didn't hit it properly as I was flying too fast to correct my aim in time. So
I pulled up behind my leader and prepared to carry out a second run.

'In the meantime, the field had come to life. Figures were rushing about
all over the place. Then a string of red pearls whizzed past my right wing.
Aha, one guy was shooting back! But this single machine gun could not
keep us from our prey. This time I got the machine I was aiming at fair
and square. It burst into flames.

'By the time we lined up for a third attack the whole field was spitting
tracer at us from every corner. It was impossible for me to hang on to my
leader's tail through this inferno. I pulled up to the right and circled
the strip.

'Oberleutnant Denk set another machine on fire, but as he began to
climb away something terrible happened. I saw his fighter take a whole
burst of quadruple flak at a height of only 200 metres. It immediately
exploded. Burning wreckage hit the ground in the middle of the field.'

Gustav Denk's final total of 67 victories (including two in the west)
resulted in the award of a posthumous Knight's Cross on 14 March. By
then another long-serving member of JG 52 had been lost. Like Denk,
1. *Staffel's* Oberfeldwebel Karl Hammerl had been with the *Geschwader*
since the beginning of the war. He had claimed his 50th kill on 19 August
1942, for which he received the Knight's Cross exactly one month later.
On 2 March 1943 he forced-landed behind enemy lines. Although
captured badly burned and transported to the Russian rear, he was yet
another semi-centurion subsequently to disappear without trace. By
coincidence, he too had achieved exactly 67 victories.

The third of the trio of JG 52's 'old guard' *Experten* to be lost early in
1943 was, in fact, one of the Luftwaffe's oldest operational fighter pilots.
32-year-old Oberfeldwebel Willi *'Altvater'* ('Old Father') Nemitz had
joined II./JG 52 during its time on the Channel coast in 1940. But he had
not opened his score sheet until after his arrival on the Russian front,
claiming a brace of DB-3 bombers downed on 3 July 1941.

Despite being of non-commissioned rank, he was appointed
Staffelkapitän of 6./JG 52 to replace the fallen Gustav Denk. And on
11 March 1943 Oberfeldwebel Nemitz was awarded the Knight's Cross
for his 54 Russian front victories to date. Over the next four weeks he
would increase that total to 81, before finally falling victim to Soviet
fighters near Anapa, in the Caucasus, on 11 April.

On that day a group of infantrymen in the frontlines reported seeing a
single Bf 109 dive out of the clouds and bore straight into the ground
without making any apparent attempt to level out. The machine had
buried itself four metres deep into the sandy soil. The pilot's identity was
established when a recovery team discovered the Knight's Cross that
'Old Father' Nemitz had worn for exactly one month.

It is indicative of just how thinly stretched the Luftwaffe's fighter arm
had by now become that only one of the nine other Russian front semi-
centurions lost between January and May 1943 actually fell in central
Russia. Of the rest, six had already been withdrawn from the east
altogether for service elsewhere, and two were operating in the Arctic
(of which more anon). The sole casualty on the main eastern front was
Oberleutnant Helmut Haberda, *Staffelkapitän* of 5./JG 52, who was
brought down by Soviet quadruple flak while carrying out a low-level

. . . before being killed over the Caucasus. Although reportedly promoted posthumously to leutnant, Willi Nemitz's rank is still given as oberfeldwebel on his grave marker (right). Close examination of the original print also shows that – contrary to post-war records – the date of his loss is given as *10* April 1943!

attack southwest of Krimskaya on 8 May. His final score of 58 sufficed to earn him a posthumous German Cross in Gold on 2 August.

During that same January-May period, however, at least eight more pilots had topped the 50 mark in the east. One of them was 4./JG 3's Feldwebel Kurt Ebener, who was awarded the Knight's Cross on 7 April for his current total of 52 kills. Some 35 of that number had been claimed under appalling conditions during the depths of the recent winter over and around Stalingrad, and had made Ebener the most successful of all the pilots who had volunteered for the Pitomnik defence *Staffel*.

There were no new semi-centurions in June 1943, and only one loss. Like his late *Gruppenkommandeur* 'Gaudi' Krafft, Oberfeldwebel Heinz Leber of I./JG 51 was flying an Fw 190 when he was shot down at low level by Soviet anti-aircraft gunners north of Mtsensk, near Orel, on 1 June. The great majority of his 54 victories, however, beginning with an I-16 despatched on 2 July 1941, had been claimed on Bf 109s before the *Gruppe* converted to the Focke-Wulf. Heinz Leber's promotion to leutnant, like his Knight's Cross (not announced until February 1944!), was posthumous.

The relative dearth of activity throughout June was very much the calm before the proverbial storm. And on this occasion the storm was to be Hitler's third Russian front summer offensive. Since retaking Stalingrad, the Red Army had been pushing forwards on all fronts. Nowhere had they advanced further than around the town of Kursk, an important railway junction connecting Moscow with the Ukraine. Here they occupied a huge salient, or 'bulge', that projected some 100 kilometres deep into the German front.

Hitler's aim was to pinch off this bulge by simultaneous attacks from north and south, and then destroy the enemy forces trapped inside it in order to gain a breathing space from the constant Soviet pressure, and give himself more time to build up his own strength. But the Red Army knew of the German plan, and had packed the bulge with troops and armour.

Launched on 5 July 1943, Operation *Zitadelle* quickly developed into the largest tank battle in military history. Air activity revolved principally around the tank-busting aircraft deployed by both sides. But Luftwaffe fighters were also present in considerable strength, and their main task

Some 35 of Kurt Ebener's 52 Russian front victories were claimed as a feldwebel while flying with the *Platzschutzstaffel Pitomnik*. This later studio portrait of Leutnant Ebener shows to advantage his Knight's Cross and the German Cross in Gold, both awarded in the spring of 1943

was to protect their own armour from the swarms of Soviet *Shturmoviks* prowling above the battlefield. On the northern edge of the salient were three *Gruppen* of JG 51, currently all equipped with Fw 190s. On the southern flank were the *Gustavs* of II. and III./JG 3, plus those of I. and III./JG 52.

The most successful pilot of the brief, but bloody, battle of Kursk was 8./JG 51's Oberfeldwebel Hubert Strassl, who downed 15 enemy machines on the opening day and then added that number again over the next 72 hours, before being killed in action on 8 July. This unparalleled string of successes would result in a posthumous Knight's Cross on 12 November 1943. Although Strassl was flying the Fw 190 when he was lost, almost a third of his final total of 67 Soviet aircraft destroyed had been claimed during earlier service on Bf 109s.

Two non-commissioned semi-centurions of III./JG 52, Oberfeldwebel Edmund Rossmann and Feldwebel Wilhelm Hauswirth, were each credited with a trio of victories apiece on 5 July. Hauswirth was reported missing after being hit by Soviet flak later that same day. His score of 54 did not suffice for a Knight's Cross, but the award of a German Cross in Gold (presumably posthumous) would be announced on 23 July.

On 9 July the highly experienced Rossmann had been ordered to lead a *Schwarm* (section of four aircraft) on an early morning weather reconnaissance flight of the southern flank battle area. Take-off was scheduled for 0300 hrs German time, but one of the pilots had trouble starting his engine. The other three somehow became separated, for the late starter – about eight minutes behind, and trying unsuccessfully to catch up – heard Oberfeldwebel Rossmann on the R/T ordering them to rendezvous at 1000 metres over Byelgorod.

Oberfeldwebel Edmund 'Paule' Rossmann (with Knight's Cross) and fellow pilots of III./JG 52 are glad of the shade provided by the wing of a transport Ju 52/3m during one of the *Gruppe's* many moves throughout the baking summer months of 1943 on the southern sector

None of the three returned to base. Accounts differ as to exactly what happened. One official source states that all three came down behind enemy lines and were taken prisoner. Another maintains that one pilot was killed and only two captured, with Rossmann deliberately putting down in Soviet-held territory in a failed attempt to rescue Feldwebel Ernst Lohberg, who had been forced to make an emergency landing. It would have been an act typical of the unassuming, but deeply caring, 93-victory 'Paule' Rossmann. His self-sacrifice would cost him more than six years of Soviet captivity.

The savage fighting around Kursk resulted in the loss not only of a large number of veteran NCOs – the true backbone of nearly every *Jagdgruppe* – but also of several equally experienced and valuable unit leaders. Among the latter was Major Rudolf Resch, the *Gruppenkommandeur* of IV./JG 51, who was shot down near Orel on 11 July. 'Rudi' Resch had seen combat in Spain with the *Legion Condor* and been wounded during the Battle of Britain. Some 73 of his final total of 94 kills – starting with the first, an SB-2 claimed on the opening day of *Barbarossa* – had been scored with JG 52 prior to his posting to JG 51 and conversion onto the Fw 190.

The day after the loss of Major Resch, the Soviets launched a major counter-offensive in the rear of the German troops engaged against the northern edge of the salient. The danger of half his own attacking force being encircled, together with the news just in from the Mediterranean of the Anglo-American landings on Sicily, completely unnerved Hitler. On 13 July, against the advice of his generals, he ordered that the Kursk operation be broken off. And four days later he began large-scale withdrawals of his forces from the area.

The *Führer's* abrupt change of mind did not come in time to save Major Wolfgang Ewald, the *Gruppenkommandeur* of III./JG 3, whose *Gustav* was brought down by Russian flak northeast of Byelgorod on 14 July. Ewald took to his parachute, but was to spend many years in captivity. He too had begun his operational career in Spain, where, like 'Rudi' Resch, he had been credited with one kill. His first two wartime victories had been scored in the west with I./JG 52, with the remaining 71 being claimed against the Soviets.

The battle of Stalingrad has gone down in history as the turning point of the war between Germany and the Soviet Union. But it was Kursk that marked the true reversal of fortunes on the Russian front, for even after Stalingrad, the Wehrmacht had been able to recover sufficiently to mount *Zitadelle* just six months later. And if not of the same magnitude as 1941's advance on Moscow, or the 1942 drive down into the Caucasus, the Battle of Kursk in the summer of 1943 was unarguably a major strategic offensive. There would never be anything like it on the same scale in the east again.

In the immediate aftermath of *Zitadelle*, the remaining *Gruppen* of JG 3, like JGs 27, 53 and 77 before them, were withdrawn from the Russian front (although in their case not for service in the Mediterranean, but in defence of the Reich). Thus, of the seven *Jagdgeschwader* that had supported the launch of *Barbarossa* just over two years earlier, less than half now remained to cover the 22-month-long retreat of the German army back to the streets of Berlin.

Legion Condor veteran and 94-victory Russian front *Experte* Major Rudolf Resch, *Gruppenkommandeur* of IV./JG 51, was shot down over the northern flank of the Kursk salient at the height of Operation *Zitadelle*

ARCTIC SIDESHOW

While the fortunes of the *Jagdgruppen* fighting on the three main sectors of the Russian front waxed and waned, there was another almost entirely separate – and much more static – war being waged far to the north of them.

The opening months of the campaign above the Arctic Circle were fought by a miscellany of units before a flurry of redesignations saw the piecemeal emergence of JG 5 proper during 1942. This *Geschwader* was somewhat unusual

in that it faced two ways at once. One half of it was employed in defending the western coast of Norway against attack by the RAF (and USAAF), while the other half was engaged against the land and naval air forces of the Soviet Union primarily over the White Sea area and along the strategically vital Murmansk railway line. The latter took supplies delivered by the Allied Arctic convoys down into central Russia.

Despite this diversity of tasks, JG 5 produced a formidable number of high-scoring *Experten* (or at least those *Gruppen* operating in the eastern parts did). In addition to a handful of truly stellar performers who racked up three-figure totals, there were at least half-a-dozen semi-centurions among their ranks.

One of the first to come to prominence was 6./JG 5's Feldwebel Rudolf 'Rudi' Müller. He was credited with five Russian-flown Hurricanes downed over Kola Bay on 23 April 1942. In less than two months his score had risen to 46, for which he was awarded the Knight's Cross on 19 June. And he had more than doubled that total again – to a final score of 94 – before he was himself lost on 19 April 1943.

On the morning of that date, 'Rudi' Müller, by now an oberfeldwebel and currently JG 5's highest scorer, was piloting one of the six Bf 109s that took off from Salmijärvi, in northern Finland, for a *freie Jagd* sweep of the Murmansk region. They had been warned to keep a special eye on the Soviet fighter base at Vaenga, on the eastern shore of Kola Bay. And with good reason, for approximately 40 enemy aircraft rose to intercept them.

A fierce dogfight developed. At least one Red Air Force Airacobra was sent down, but another latched onto the tail of Müller's *Gustav* and got in an effective burst. Müller tried to escape by diving away in a steep spiral, but his machine was too badly damaged and he was forced to belly-land on the surface of a frozen lake. While the battle continued to rage overhead, his victor is described as having 'put down alongside the stricken Messerschmitt'. But of Müller there was no sign – just a set of snow-shoe tracks heading off into the tundra.

Cap askew, personal victory stick well in evidence, Feldwebel Rudolf Müller is congratulated on achieving II./JG 5's 500th collective kill. This photograph was taken at Petsamo in June 1942

Snapshot of the ebullient 'Rudi' Müller wearing the Knight's Cross awarded on 19 June 1942 for his then 46 victories. Is he practising a new kind of salute – or simply letting the photographer know what he thinks of him?

'Rudi' Müller remained at large behind enemy lines for several days before finally being captured. Like so many others who disappeared into Soviet captivity, his ultimate fate is unknown. One statement released long after the war asserted that he had been killed while trying to escape in October 1943, but there were also reported sightings of him in a Russian gaol as late as 1947, and one of the many rumours circulating about him at that time among other German prisoners was to the effect that 'Rudi is serving as a flying instructor for the Ivan'.

Although Oberfeldwebel Rudolf Müller had been JG 5's most successful pilot at the time of his loss, he had not been the first future semi-centurion of the *Geschwader* to receive the Knight's Cross. That had gone to his *Staffelkapitän*, Oberleutnant Horst Carganico, back on 25 September 1941 when 6./JG 5 had been operating under its previous guise as 1./JGr.z.b.V. Petsamo. Carganico was decorated for his then total of 27 aircraft destroyed, five of which he had claimed prior to *Barbarossa*. He reached his half-century in June 1942, by which time he had been appointed *Gruppenkommandeur* of II./JG 5.

In March 1944 Major Carganico was posted back to Germany to assume command of I./JG 5. After long service in Norway, this *Gruppe* had recently taken up Defence of the Reich duties. It had already lost one *Kommandeur* to US fighters, and on 27 May 1944 it lost a second when Horst Carganico was killed while attempting a forced landing after his machine had been damaged in action against the USAAF's Eighth Air Force over France. He had apparently added just ten more to his total over the two years that had elapsed since his 50th in mid-1942.

Another 50+ *Experte* among the NCOs of 6./JG 5 who, like 'Rudi' Müller, was to claim all his victories on the Arctic front was Oberfeldwebel Albert Brunner. He had been serving as a flying instructor before joining the *Staffel* in the spring of 1942, and it took him the best part of five months to achieve his first dozen kills. Then, on 4 September, after downing his 14th, Brunner had to bale out over enemy territory. He reappeared four days later, having made his way back on foot.

Due to a variety of reasons – enemy action, the often foul weather and the almost featureless landscape that made navigation such a problem – it is perhaps not surprising that a considerable number of JG 5's pilots had

Feldwebel Müller's 'Yellow 3' (see colour profile 6) displaying the 50 kill bars that gained him entry to the ranks of the Russian front's semi-centurions. This photo was also taken at Petsamo in late June 1942

Another Arctic front *Experte* to reach his half-century at the end of June 1942 was Müller's CO, Hauptmann Horst Carganico, *Gruppenkommandeur* of II./JG 5

A barefoot Horst Carganico returns to Petsamo on 23 July after the first of his two day-long treks back from behind enemy lines. These incidents would subsequently be recorded in some detail on the fuselage of one of his later *Gustavs* (see *Aircraft of the Aces 37*, page 50)

'Rudi' Müller in uncharacteristically sombre mood after being hit in the left arm and face by glass splinters from his canopy, which was shattered by enemy fire during a Bf 110 escort mission on 21 August 1942. Acting-*Staffelkapitän* Leutnant Heinrich Ehrler (a future 200+ *Experte*) obviously commiserates

Killed in action on 7 May 1943, 6./JG 5's Oberfeldwebel Albert Brunner would, unusually, be honoured with both a posthumous Knight's Cross *and* German Cross in Gold for his 53 Arctic front victories

to take to their parachutes or make emergency landings behind enemy lines. Nor is it surprising that so many of them subsequently got back (Horst Carganico managed it on at least two occasions). They were helped both by the nature of the terrain which, although extremely harsh, was barren and all but uninhabited, and by the type of campaign being fought in the Arctic.

Enemy troops were relatively thin on the ground in the rear areas. Most were manning the elaborate system of frontline trenches that had grown up over the months of static warfare in the far north, these being more reminiscent of Flanders in 1914-18 than the present conflict.

On 4 April 1943 Oberfeldwebel Brunner was again brought down over enemy territory, but this time he hardly had to walk a step, as he later recounted to a war correspondent;

'We were given the order for an emergency scramble. The enemy was carrying out a low-level attack on a neighbouring airfield. As we approached it, I managed to bag a Tomahawk. Then, suddenly, we were faced by a large gaggle of Airacobras. I took on four of them and soon managed to shoot down two. Aircraft were diving, turning and twisting at low level above and between the tundra hills. But I tackled my fourth opponent head-on. We flew straight at each other and must have opened fire at the same

time (both machines were hit, the Russian disappearing eastwards trailing smoke). Suddenly my crate was making all kinds of funny noises, the engine stopped and bits were flying off the wings and tail. Nothing for it but to put her down as quickly as possible!

'Fortunately, I spotted a frozen lake very close by and succeeded in making a smooth belly landing on its icy surface. After I had set my aircraft on fire, I simply awaited developments, for I knew my *Staffel* comrades would come looking for me, and find me.

'In the meantime, a reconnaissance patrol of our own mountain troops who had been watching the air battle discovered me. They immediately assumed responsibility for protecting me against any nasty surprises – the nearest Soviet strong points weren't all that far away.

'Then two '109s that had been sent to search for the spot where I had come down appeared overhead, and not long afterwards – to the amazement of the troops – a Fieseler "Storch", piloted by my comrade Rudi Müller, landed right next to us to pick me up and take me home.'

Rudi Müller had been just in time. As the 'Storch' flew off, a firefight developed between the German patrol and some Red Army troops who had arrived on the scene. By a strange coincidence, another future semi-centurion, 7./JG 5's Unteroffizier Helmut Neumann, was also rescued by a 'Storch' on this date after being brought down near Petsamo. But there was to be no such succour for Rudi Müller when he himself belly-landed on that frozen lake east of Murmansk just over a fortnight later.

The action on 4 April had taken Oberfeldwebel Brunner's score to 42. He would add 11 more enemy aircraft to this total during the course of the next month, before his luck finally deserted him on 7 May. On that date he was part of the fighter escort for a force of Luftwaffe bombers and fighter-bombers attacking the port of Murmansk. After claiming his 53rd, and final, Soviet victim, Brunner's own machine was hit. Although

Standing by the tailplane of his 'Yellow 10' at Petsamo on 30 June 1942, just four months into his operational career, Unteroffizier Hans Döbrich seems to be wondering how many more kills – over and above the 18 already booked on the rudder of the Bf 109F seen here – will be required to finish carving his still more than half-empty victory stick . . .

. . . a year later and Feldwebel Döbrich perches in the cockpit of his winter-camouflaged *Gustav* with a score nearing the 60 mark. Note the sandy soil of the dispersal area – more like the desert than the Arctic!

JG 5 had begun converting to
Bf 109Gs in the winter of 1942–43.
This strikingly camouflaged
machine, seen at Petsamo early in
1943, is one of the last *Friedrichs* of
III./JG 5 – identifiable by the *Gruppe*
symbol (a large disc) visible on the
rear fuselage . . .

. . . the change-over did not always
go smoothly. A brand-new *Gustav* –
in overall white finish and still
bearing factory-applied codes – has
come to grief on the edge of the
runway at Alarkutti, in Finland, as
a Ju 88 takes off in the background

JG 5's new mounts did not retain
their pristine white paint jobs for
long, as witness this decidedly
grubby example being operated by
the *Gruppenstab* of III./JG 5 out of
Petsamo. Of more interest, perhaps,
are the local beasts of burden. While
most *Jagdgruppen* on the main
sectors depended on sturdy little
Russian panje ponies for hauling
stores and supplies during severe
weather conditions, in the Arctic,
such duties were often performed
by reindeer!

he managed to bale out, he was too low for his parachute to open
properly. Oberfeldwebel Albert Brunner was honoured with a post
humous Knight's Cross.

The fourth Knight's Cross awarded to a semi-centurion of 6./JG 5, the
acknowledged *Experten-Staffel* of the Arctic front, went to Feldwebel
Hans Döbrich on 19 September 1943 for a total then standing at 52. He
too had joined the *Staffel* early in 1942, and in six months claimed 18
victories before it became his turn to make the almost obligatory walk
back from behind enemy lines. In Döbrich's case, this developed into a
week-long odyssey.

It had been on 19 July 1942 that 6./JG 5 was despatched on a *freie Jagd*
sweep of the Murmansk area. Here, it ran into a hornets' nest of Soviet
fighters – Hurricanes, Airacobras and Kittyhawks – disturbed by a dive-
bombing raid on the port by Ju 87s
only minutes earlier. The *Staffel*
claimed four of the enemy. A P-40
provided Döbrich with his 19th kill,
but then his own 'Yellow 9' was hit
in the radiator. With his engine on
fire he baled out 20 kilometres west
of the Soviet fighter field at Mur-
maschi. He remained on the missing
list until turning up at Petsamo after
a seven-day trek across the tundra.

Hans Döbrich was brought down
by enemy fighters on at least two

further occasions. The third time, in July 1943, resulted in his being rescued badly wounded from the waters of Petsamo Fjord by a German patrol boat. One source maintains that this put an end to his operational career. But this does not tally with his subsequent Knight's Cross and final Arctic front total of 65 (plus another 19 unconfirmed).

The scores of the last two far northern semi-centurions are even less cut-and-dried. Both were *Staffelkapitäne* in the final months of the war, long after German forces had been obliged to leave Finland for Norway, and at a time when their units operated both the Bf 109 and the Fw 190.

Unteroffizier Helmut Neumann had joined 7./JG 5 in August 1942. It took almost a year, until 22 July 1943, before he claimed his first kill. He then began to score slowly, but regularly, his successes including an Airacobra in August and a pair of Kittyhawks in September. By August 1944 his Arctic victories numbered 49. It was in this month that Neumann, by now promoted to leutnant and serving as the *Gruppen-Adjutant* of III./JG 5, was transferred to IV. *Gruppe* as the *Staffelkapitän* of 14./JG 5, which he would lead until April 1945.

When Finland concluded a separate armistice with the Soviet Union in September 1944, and demanded that all German troops leave Finnish soil, IV./JG 5 was still based at Salmijärvi, southwest of Petsamo. Here it would remain until October before retiring, via Nautsi, first to Kirkenes and then to Banak, in northern Norway, where it continued to oppose the Russians. Early in November, the *Gruppe* was then transferred, minus its aircraft, down to Stavanger, in the far south of Norway, for re-equipment with new *Gustavs*.

For the rest of the war IV./JG 5 would operate solely against the RAF flying in from across the North Sea. It is not known whether Helmut Neumann claimed any successes during these closing weeks. At least one source states that all 62 of the victories that earned him the Knight's Cross on 12 March 1945 had been gained against the Soviets.

The details of Leutnant Rudi Linz's late-war career are similarly vague. He too had been appointed a *Staffelkapitän* in the summer of 1944, taking over 12./JG 5 in July. Towards the end of the year his score was standing at 55. Linz's 12. *Staffel* formed part of III./JG 5, and the laying down of Finnish arms had likewise resulted in this *Gruppe's* withdrawal from the Petsamo area to Kirkenes and Banak, fighting the Russians all the while. In November III./JG 5 had then retired to Bardufoss to begin conversion onto the Fw 190. The following month it joined IV. *Gruppe* in southern Norway, with 12./JG 5 taking up residence at Herdla.

Unlike Helmut Neumann, however, Rudi Linz is believed to have claimed several RAF victories during the winter of 1944-45 while defending the Norwegian coastline with his *Staffel* of Focke-Wulfs. The last of them (possibly a Mustang of No 65 Sqn) he shot down near Meistad on 9 February 1945, before losing his own life in the same engagement. He was awarded a posthumous Knight's Cross in March for a total of 70 enemy aircraft destroyed.

So ended the Luftwaffe fighter arm's involvement in the Arctic war – not with a bang, but with a whimper. Apart from the final withdrawal down the length of Norway, it had been a remarkably static campaign. Not so on the main Russian front, where the long retreat from the battlefields of Kursk was only just beginning.

Claiming 62 victories in total, Leutnant Helmut Neumann served as *Staffelkapitän* of 14./JG 5 from August 1944 until April 1945. He is pictured here towards the end of his tenure of office, wearing both the German Cross in Gold and Knight's Cross (awarded in January and March 1945 respectively)

Another late-war *Staffelkapitän* of JG 5, Leutnant Rudi Linz took over the re-formed 7./JG 5 in July 1944. Like Neumann, he too received the German Cross in Gold on 1 January 1945, but in his case the Knight's Cross that followed in March was posthumous. He had been killed in action against RAF Mustangs on 9 February

STEPS RETRACED

The immediate aftermath of *Zitadelle* brought very little relief to those units actively engaged in the area. Between Hitler's ordering the abandonment of the twin offensives at Kursk on 13 July and the end of that month, five more semi-centurions would be lost. All were flying Fw 190s.

The first, Leutnant Günther Scheel of 3./JG 54, had been killed in action on 16 July after he had rammed a Yak-9 during a low-level dogfight and his own 'Yellow 8' crashed behind enemy lines near Orel. Scheel had only joined JG 54

in the spring, and in less than six months had been credited with 71 Soviet aircraft destroyed. But as the *Staffeln* of I./JG 54 had been rotated back to East Prussia during February 1943 to exchange their Bf 109s for Focke-Wulfs, there is every likelihood that Günther Scheel's entire operational career had been spent on the latter type (which, in passing, would make him a strong contender for being the Russian front's first Fw 190 semi-centurion).

July's four other casualties, however, had all started out on Messerschmitts. The diminutive Leutnant Josef 'Pepi' Jennewein, for example, had previously flown the Bf 109 with both IV. and I./JG 51, although he admittedly achieved his greatest run of success during the first half of 1943 (on the Fw 190) before he too was lost over Soviet-held territory near Orel on 26 July. Jennewein would be awarded a posthumous Knight's Cross on 5 December 1943 for his final total of 81 Russian front victories.

Three days after 'Pepi' Jennewein went down, I./JG 51 lost another of its long-serving members when Oberfeldwebel Wilhelm Theimann of 1. *Staffel* was reported missing. All but one of his 55 kills had been achieved against the Red Air Force, starting with an SB-2 claimed on the opening day of *Barbarossa*. His earlier victories on the Bf 109 had contributed in no small part to the award of the German Cross in Gold on 31 March 1943.

The month's last two fatalities were both sustained on 30 July. Leutnant Otto Tange was another veteran NCO who had been with II./JG 51 since 1940. With three western kills already to his credit, he too had cut his Russian front teeth on the SB-2, claiming three on 25 June 1941. Since that date Tange had added a further 62 Soviet aircraft to his tally. Recently transferred to the *Stabsstaffel* of JG 51 (see *Osprey Aviation Elite Units 22 - Jagdgeschwader 51 'Mölders'* for full details of this 'one-off' *Staffel*), Leutnant Otto Tange was killed when his 'Black 4' took a direct

Judging from the melting snow underfoot and the Fw 190 being serviced in the background, Leutnant Josef Jennewein's comrades in I./JG 51 must have considered him deserving of the Knight's Cross by the early spring of 1943 (at a time when a total of 50 kills was the approximate benchmark). So, with nothing forthcoming from official sources, they decided to make a large wooden one of their own to present to him! Unfortunately, 'Pepi' Jennewein never did get to wear the real thing. He was lost on 26 July 1943 when his overall total was standing at 86, which finally resulted in a posthumous award over four months later

JG 51's Leutnant Otto Tange had been wearing his Knight's Cross (awarded for 41 victories) for more than 16 months by the time he was brought down by a direct flak hit just four days after the loss of Jennewein

hit from enemy flak and crashed in flames into a Russian village southwest of Bolkhov.

Hauptmann Heinrich Jung's operational career had also begun in 1940 when he joined JG 54. But it was nearly a year before he was credited with his first kill – identified simply as a 'Douglas' – in Russia on 13 October 1941. He was appointed *Kommandeur* of II./JG 54 in February 1943, just as that *Gruppe* was exchanging its Bf 109s for Fw 190s. He was lost in a dogfight east of Mga on the Leningrad front moments after claiming a Lavochkin La-5 as his 68th, and final, Soviet victim. A posthumous Knight's Cross followed on 12 November 1943.

Apart from the posthumous German Cross in Gold for II./JG 52's Oberleutnant Helmut Haberda mentioned earlier, only three awards were announced in August – all on the last day of the month. Feldwebel Horst Forbrig and Oberfeldwebel Kurt Olsen, both of I./JG 54, also each received the German Cross in Gold. The former promoted in the meantime to leutnant, would be lost over the Normandy beachhead in June 1944 when his total was standing at 58. The latter, also by then a leutnant, is believed to have survived being shot down and wounded in the Arnhem area three months later with a final score of 54. As far as can

Hauptmann Heinrich Jung, *Gruppenkommandeur* of II./JG 54, was also killed in action on 30 July 1943. Like Jennewein's, his posthumous Knight's Cross would not be announced for several months . . .

. . . which is why there is no mention of it on this memorial to the fallen at II./JG 54's base at Siverskaya. Heinrich Jung's marker is the broad black propeller blade (with damaged tip) immediately below the cross. In contrast to the *Jagdgruppen* on the southern sector, which were constantly on the move, JG 54 led an almost sedentary existence in the north during the long drawn out siege of Leningrad. An indication of this is provided by the narrow polished blade to the right of Jung's. It is that of Knight's Cross winner Hauptmann Joachim Wandel, *Kapitän* of 5. *Staffel* – lost almost ten months earlier!

be ascertained, all these successes were achieved on the Russian front, but it must be assumed that many were claimed while flying the Fw 190.

No uncertainty surrounds the third decoration to be announced on 31 August 1943 – the Oak Leaves to Major Hartmann Grasser for his 103 victories. II./JG 51, which Grasser had commanded from September 1941 to June 1943, was the only *Gruppe* of JG 51 to fly Bf 109s throughout the war. And although Major Grasser had led his unit to North Africa late in 1942 (where he would claim his last 11 victories), all 85 of his Russian front kills had been scored on the Bf 109.

But such outward symbols of success were more than overshadowed by August's five losses. The first of these had been Oberleutnant Hans Götz, the acting *Kommandeur* of I./JG 54, who was killed on 4 August while attacking a formation of Il-2s northeast of Karachev. Apparently hit by return fire from one of the *Shturmoviks'* rear gunners, Götz's 'Black 2' suddenly flipped onto its back and crashed inverted into a forest, exploding in flames on impact. All but three of Götz's final total of 82 had been scored on the Russian front.

Three days later, another Fw 190 was brought down in the Karachev area. This was 'Brown 5' of 3./JG 51, flown by Leutnant Heinrich Höfemeier, which had fallen victim to Soviet anti-aircraft fire. 'Tubby' Höfemeier had opened his score sheet with a quartet of the omnipresent SB-2s during the opening hours of *Barbarossa*. That score sheet had since lengthened to just four short of a century, making him I./JG 51's topmost *Experte* at the time of his loss.

On that same 7 August, II./JG 52 had lost one of *its* high scorers down over the Black Sea coast. Fahnenjunker-Oberfeldwebel (Senior NCO Officer Candidate) Werner Quast had first joined 4./JG 52 in 1941. Since that time he had taken a steady toll of Russian aircraft. But perhaps his most unusual 'kill' had been the sinking of a motor torpedo boat of the Soviet Black Sea Fleet on 20 April 1943. The then Feldwebel Quast wrote his own account of how it came about;

'I had already spent some three-quarters of an hour on a fruitless *freie Jagd* mission over the Gelendzhik area of the Caucasian Black Sea coast. Not a single opponent had put in an appearance so far. I knew I could remain for another 15 minutes, but you tend to get over-confident flying around for such a long time in the blue with nothing happening.

'Then I remembered the gunboat that I had seen putting out from Gelendzhik harbour when I first arrived. I had spotted it because of the large white bow wave it was making. Later it lay stopped, and I would no longer have noticed it if two other fighters had not just then happened to dive down on it and carry out a low-level strafing run.

'Now I started to search for it again. It had picked up full speed again, and I had just flown across its wake, which I momentarily mistook for a breaking wave, when suddenly it dawned on me – the boat! Should I, or shouldn't I? Before I had time to think, I had dived down from 3000 metres and was racing just above the water head-on straight towards its bow.

'The boat quickly grew in my gun-sight, and equally quickly grew the feeling inside me that I had let myself in for something really idiotic. I was attacking with the sun at my back, but I had already been seen. Tracers from the boat's 20 mm flak whooshed towards me and flew past to left

Pictured early in 1943, shortly after I./JG 54 re-equipped with the Fw 190, Oberleutnant Hans Götz was killed in action on 4 August 1943 – just 24 hours after he had been appointed acting-*Kommandeur* of the *Gruppe*

and right of my cockpit, as did the smaller pearls of machine gun fire. I felt a moment of cowardice.

'Shouldn't I just break off the attack and turn away? But then I got my feelings back under control – "You've cooked this soup yourself, so now you'd better ladle it out yourself!" So I held my course straight for the bow of the boat and fired and fired!

'While still on my approach run, which only lasted a matter of seconds, I could already see explosions on the ship and a fire starting. Then I was low over the boat and away while my *Kaczmarek* (wingman), who had not followed me down in the dive, flew past above.

'My attack had been carried out in the direction of the land, and so I pulled a tight, low-level turn to get back out to sea, and at the same time began to climb.

'At an altitude of 2000 metres, I circled my victim and saw black and white clouds of smoke billowing out of it. I asked my *Kaczmarek*, "Can you see that the boat's burning?" He thought the white smoke was mist, and answered, "No, the boat is under way again!" I ordered him to come down and have a closer look while I covered him. This convinced him, and he confirmed my observation. After that we flew to Gelendzhik again, but there was still no enemy air activity in the area.

'On our way back to base we flew over the gunboat again, which was lying stopped level with Kabardinka. Hardly had we sighted it when a huge sheet of flame tore the black smoke apart. As this slowly dispersed the boat had disappeared and three figures could be seen in the water. Now it was high time to head for home.'

Just over a month later, on 30 May, Feldwebel Quast reached his half-century. And in the ten weeks that followed he added 34 more. The final four he claimed on 7 August, but the last took 'Quax' Quast down with it. A unit diarist recorded;

'Soviet assault aircraft were attacking our ferries yet again. We only had four machines in the air – the *Schwarmführer* was Oberfeldebel Quast – and it was a case of "go get 'em!", for our supply routes had to be kept secure! Four enemy fighters had already been shot down, three by Quast alone. Now he's after his fourth victim – one of the *Shturmoviks* – opens fire, hits it, and tries to weave away underneath the enemy machine, which is already on its way down – too late! The Russian and the '109 both go into the sea together. "Quax" was observed being rescued by a Soviet ship and so is on his way into captivity.'

Werner Quast's Knight's Cross would be announced on 31 December 1943. He would remain a prisoner of the Russians for six years before being returned to Germany in 1949.

On 8 August, just 24 hours after Quast's capture, 9./JG 52 also lost one of its veteran NCO pilots. Oberfeldwebel Karl Steffen had

Another of August 1943's casualties was Oberfeldwebel Karl Steffen of 9./JG 52, who was reported missing four days after Hans Götz was shot down. He is seen here on the right in the foreground, marching past assembled groundcrew on the day he was awarded the Knight's Cross. The other officers to his right are Major Hubertus von Bonin (left), *Gruppenkommandeur* of III./JG 52, and Unteroffizier Karl Gratz (future 121-victory Russian front *Experte*, who received his Knight's Cross on the same occasion)

claimed his 50th kill on 3 August. Nine more were to be added over the next five days before Steffen was reported missing after a forced landing behind enemy lines southwest of Byelgorod. And just six days later still, on 14 August, yet another of III./JG 52's semi-centurions would fail to return.

Unteroffizier Karl-Heinz Meltzer's 27th kill, scored on 4 July, had provided the *Gruppe* with its 2500th victory of the war. Coincidentally, he reached his 50th on the same date as Karl Steffen – 3 August. And in the 11 days thereafter Meltzer was credited with 24 more, taking his final total to 74 before he was himself shot down over Kharkov on 14 August.

By now the German troops' retreat westward had begun in earnest. But after August's activity, the next two months were to provide the Luftwaffe's fighter pilots with a brief period of respite. During this time only one Russian front 50+ *Experte* was lost – and even he was already serving in France.

The then Gefreiter Kurt Knappe of II./JG 51 had claimed his first success (an Ilyushin DB-3) back on 26 July 1941. He soon established himself as one of the *Gruppe's* dependable 'old guard' NCOs, being credited with his half-century on 4 October 1942. He would achieve one further kill in the east – which had won him the Knight's Cross on 3 November – before being posted to JG 2 on the Channel coast, where he was killed in action against RAF Spitfires on 3 September 1943.

There were only four awards relevant to Russian front semi-centurions during this same two-month period. All were German Crosses in Gold, and all were conferred on 17 October. One was posthumous (that honouring the achievements of Karl-Heinz Meltzer), and two of the other three went to NCO pilots of III./JG 51, both of whom would be killed in the early weeks of 1944. Only the fourth recipient, 2./JG 52's Oberleutnant Paul-Heinrich Dähne, would survive long enough to be awarded the Knight's Cross – on 6 April 1944, for his then total of 74 victories, all but the first claimed in the east – before his transfer to Reich's Defence duties. Hauptmann Dähne would lose his life on 24 April 1945 while flying Heinkel's radical He 162 light-weight jet fighter.

The final two months of 1943 did not start well. On 8 November Oberleutnant Hermann Lücke of 9./JG 51 succumbed to the burns he

And still the losses continued to rise. After earlier acting as medal bearer for a fallen comrade (Oberfeldwebel Bernhard Lausch of 8./JG 51) at the latter's burial service, Oberleutnant Hermann Lücke of 9. *Staffel* would himself succumb to injuries received during a take-off accident on 23 October 1943

had received when he was involved in a collision with another Fw 190 while taking off from Kosinki on 23 October. And three days after his death, 1./JG 54's Oberfeldwebel Anton Döbele also met his end as the result of a collision – mid-air, this time.

References differ as to the exact circumstances. One states that Döbele's 'White 11' was rammed by another German fighter over the Smolensk-Vitebsk supply highway close to the *Gruppe's* base. But JG 54 records (which contain no

A member of the famous Nowotny-*Schwarm*, 94-victory Oberfeldwebel Anton 'Toni' Döbele of 1./JG 54 (note *Staffel* standard at left) was killed in a mid-air collision on 11 November 1943

details of a comparable loss to sustain this) indicate that Döbele's machine either hit, or was hit by, a Russian *Shturmovik*. Whatever the true facts, the loss of 'Toni' Döbele brought to an end the exploits of the famed 'Nowotny-*Schwarm*' – four pilots led by the legendary Walter Nowotny, who between them had accounted for hundreds of Soviet aircraft (see *Osprey Aviation Elite Units 6 - Jagdgeschwader 54 'Grünherz'* for further details).

Although Lücke and Döbele ended their careers on Fw 190s, both had joined their respective units well before conversion to the Focke-Wulf had taken place, and thus many of their Russian front victories (totalling 81 and 94 respectively) had been gained while flying Messerschmitts. The same applied to the month's third casualty (*text continues on page 62*),

Another sombre moment as Oberfeldwebel Anton Döbele is laid to rest

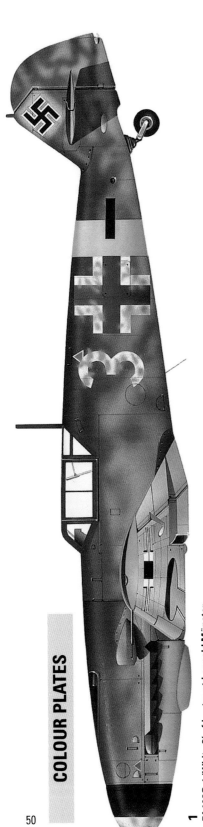

COLOUR PLATES

1
Bf 109G-4 'White 3' of Leutnant Leopold Münster,
4./JG 3, Varvarovka/Ukraine, Summer 1943

2
Bf 109F-4 'Black 6' of Oberfeldwebel Alfred Heckmann,
5./JG 3, Mariyevka/Voronezh Province, July 1942

3
Bf 109G-4 'Black Chevron and Bar' of Major Wolfgang Ewald, *Gruppenkommandeur*
III./JG 3, Gorlovka/Ukraine, January 1943

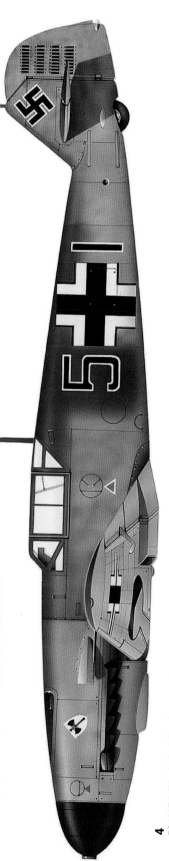

4
Bf 109F-2 'Black 5' of Oberleutnant Franz Beyer, *Staffelkapitän*
8./JG 3, Byelaya-Zerkov/Ukraine, Summer 1941

5
Bf 109F-4 'Yellow 4' of Oberfeldwebel Eberhard von Boremski,
9./JG 3, Zhuguyev/Ukraine, May 1942

6
Bf 109F-4 'Yellow 3' of Feldwebel Rudolf Müller,
6./JG 5, Petsamo/Arctic Front, June 1942

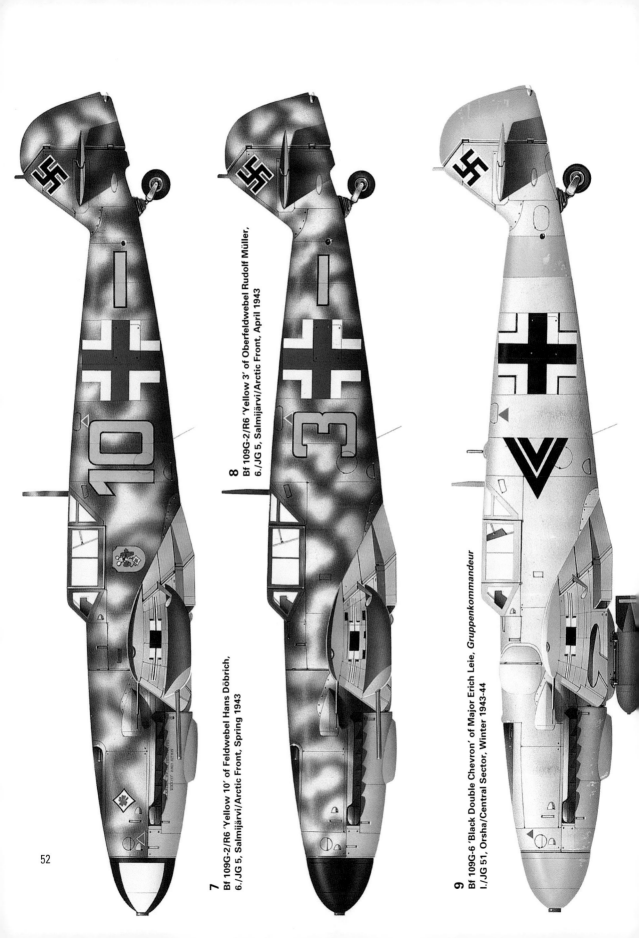

7
Bf 109G-2/R6 'Yellow 10' of Feldwebel Hans Döbrich,
6./JG 5, Salmijärvi/Arctic Front, Spring 1943

8
Bf 109G-2/R6 'Yellow 3' of Oberfeldwebel Rudolf Müller,
6./JG 5, Salmijärvi/Arctic Front, April 1943

9
Bf 109G-6 'Black Double Chevron' of Major Erich Leie, *Gruppenkommandeur*
I./JG 51, Orsha/Central Sector, Winter 1943-44

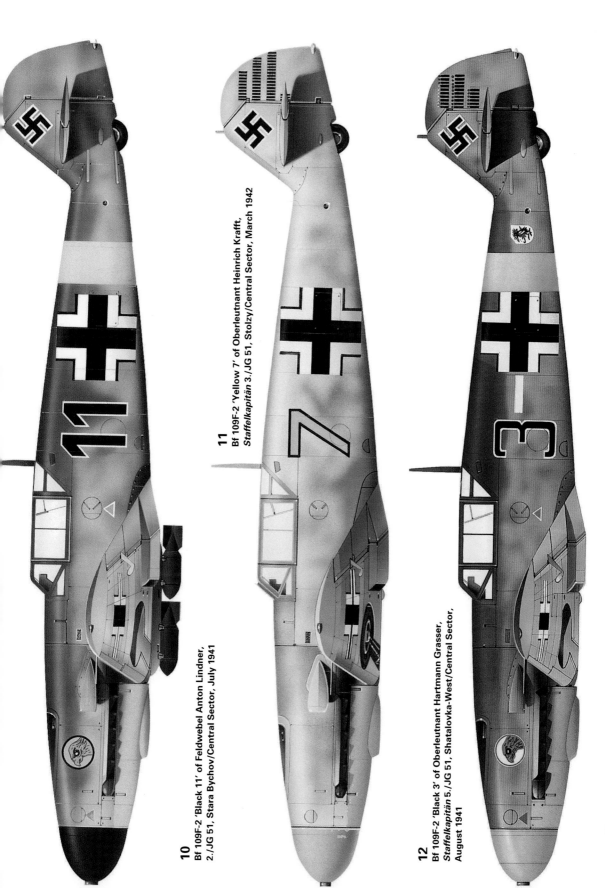

10
Bf 109F-2 'Black 11' of Feldwebel Anton Lindner,
2./JG 51, Stara Bychov/Central Sector, July 1941

11
Bf 109F-2 'Yellow 7' of Oberleutnant Heinrich Krafft,
Staffelkapitän 3./JG 51, Stolzy/Central Sector, March 1942

12
Bf 109F-2 'Black 3' of Oberleutnant Hartmann Grasser,
Staffelkapitän 5./JG 51, Shatalovka-West/Central Sector,
August 1941

53

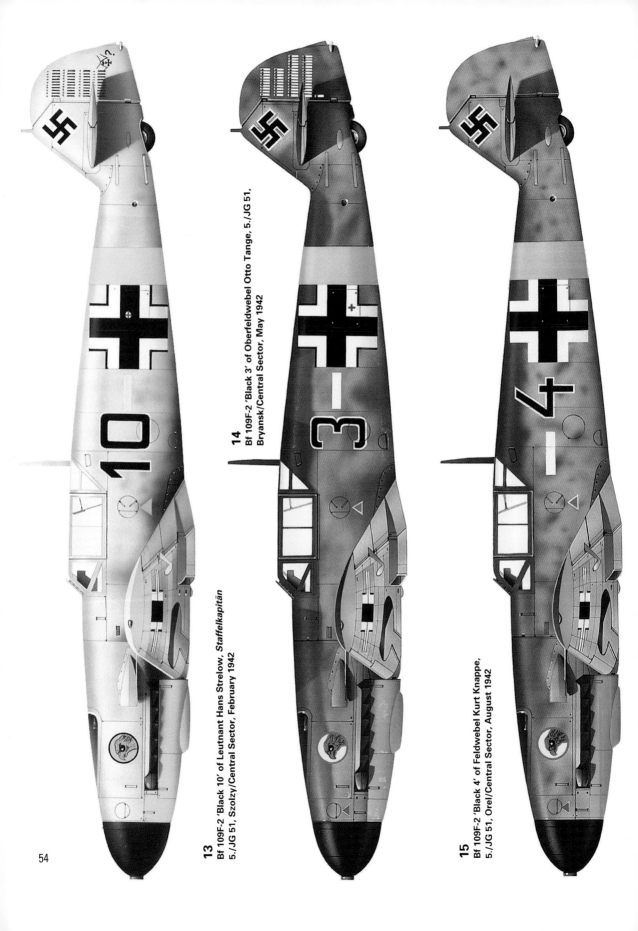

13
Bf 109F-2 'Black 10' of Leutnant Hans Strelow, *Staffelkapitän*
5./JG 51, Szolzy/Central Sector, February 1942

14
Bf 109F-2 'Black 3' of Oberfeldwebel Otto Tange, 5./JG 51,
Bryansk/Central Sector, May 1942

15
Bf 109F-2 'Black 4' of Feldwebel Kurt Knappe,
5./JG 51, Orel/Central Sector, August 1942

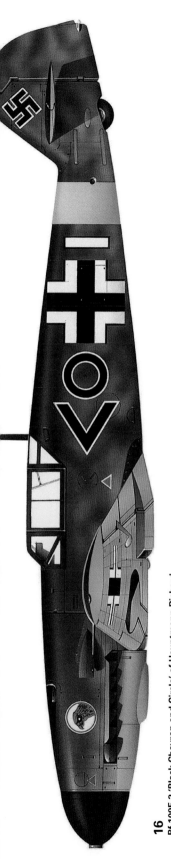

16
Bf 109F-2 'Black Chevron and Circle' of Hauptmann Richard Leppla, *Gruppenkommandeur* III./JG 51, Yuchnov/Central Sector, August 1942

17
Bf 109F-2 'Yellow 1' of Oberfeldwebel Edmund Wagner, 9./JG 51, Yuchnov/Central Sector, October 1941

18
Bf 109F-2 'Black Double Chevron' of Oberleutnant Karl-Gottfried Nordmann, *Gruppenkommandeur* IV./JG 51, Shatalovka/Central Sector, August 1941

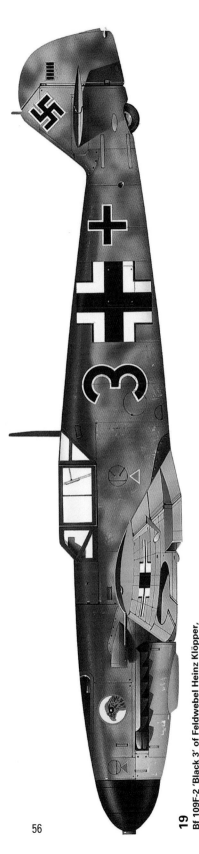

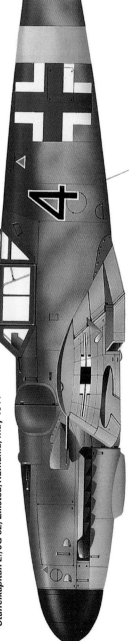

19

Bf 109F-2 'Black 3' of Feldwebel Heinz Klöpper,
11./JG 51, Minsk/Central Sector, July 1941

20

Bf 109G-2/R6 'Black Double Chevron' of Hauptmann Helmut
Bennemann, *Gruppenkommandeur* I./JG 52,
Maikop/Caucasus, October 1942

21

Bf 109G-6 'Black 4' of Oberleutnant Paul-Heinrich Dähne,
Staffelkapitän 2./JG 52, Zilistea/Rumania, May 1944

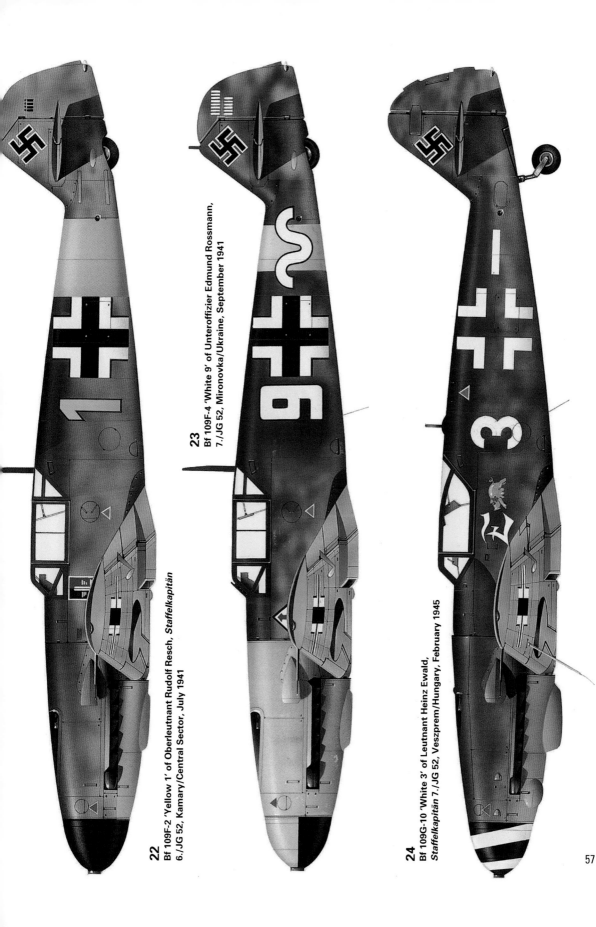

22
Bf 109F-2 'Yellow 1' of Oberleutnant Rudolf Resch, *Staffelkapitän*
6./JG 52, Kamary/Central Sector, July 1941

23
Bf 109F-4 'White 9' of Unteroffizier Edmund Rossmann,
7./JG 52, Mironovka/Ukraine, September 1941

24
Bf 109G-10 'White 3' of Leutnant Heinz Ewald,
Staffelkapitän 7./JG 52, Veszprem/Hungary, February 1945

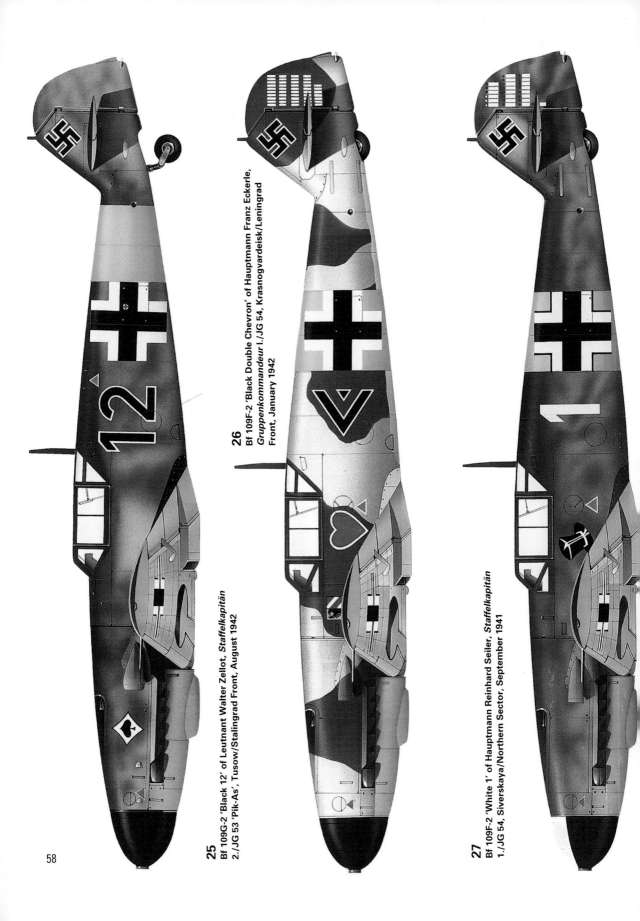

25
Bf 109G-2 'Black 12' of Leutnant Walter Zellot, *Staffelkapitän*
2./JG 53 'Pik-As', Tusow/Stalingrad Front, August 1942

26
Bf 109F-2 'Black Double Chevron' of Hauptmann Franz Eckerle,
Gruppenkommandeur I./JG 54, Krasnogvardeisk/Leningrad
Front, January 1942

27
Bf 109F-2 'White 1' of Hauptmann Reinhard Seiler, *Staffelkapitän*
1./JG 54, Siverskaya/Northern Sector, September 1941

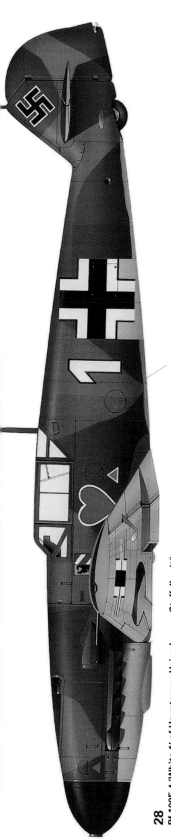

28
Bf 109F-4 'White 1' of Hauptmann Heinz Lange, *Staffelkapitän*
1./JG 54, Krasnogvardeisk/Leningrad Front, Spring 1942

29
Bf 109F-2 'Black 1' of Oberleutnant Wolfgang Späte,
Staffelkapitän 5./JG 54, Staraya-Russa/Northern Sector,
October 1941

30
Bf 109F-4 'White Double Chevron' of Hauptmann Reinhard Seiler,
Gruppenkommandeur III./JG 54, Siverskaya/Northern Sector,
Summer 1942

31
Bf 109F-4 'Black 9' of
Oberleutnant Günther Fink,
8./JG 54, Siverskaya/Northern
Sector, June 1942

32
Bf 109E-7 'White 11' of Oberleutnant Horst Carganico,
Staffelkapitän 1./JG 77, Petsamo/Arctic Front, July 1941

33
Bf 109G-2 'White Chevron/Yellow 1' of Hauptmann Kurt Ubben,
Gruppenkommandeur III./JG 77, Lyuban/Northern Sector,
September 1942

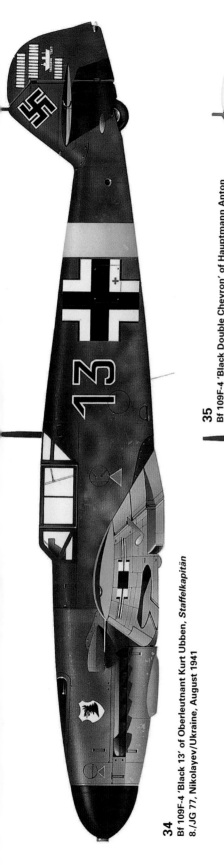

34
Bf 109F-4 'Black 13' of Oberleutnant Kurt Ubben, *Staffelkapitän*
8./JG 77, Nikolayev/Ukraine, August 1941

35
Bf 109F-4 'Black Double Chevron' of Hauptmann Anton
Mader, *Gruppenkommandeur* II./JG 77, Kastornoye/Don
Front, September 1942

36
Bf 109E-4 'Black Double Chevron' of Hauptmann Herbert Ihlefeld,
Gruppenkommandeur I.(J)/LG 2, Jassy/Rumania, July 1941

Oberleutnant Heinrich Klöpper, who, although reported missing on Defence of the Reich operations (on 29 November), had claimed the bulk of his 78 earlier Russian front victims on the Bf 109, prior to IV./JG 51's six-month stint on Focke-Wulfs.

Two more Russian front semi-centurions, both ex-JG 52, would be brought down in December 1943 after being transferred to other theatres. Oberleutnant Ernst Süss had added just two further successes to his Russian tally of 66 when he was killed in action over the Reich on 20 December. Feldwebel Wilhelm Freuwörth had likewise been credited with two western kills (a pair of Spitfires to add to his single Blenheim of 1941 and 55 intervening Soviet victories) after exchanging the rigours of Stalingrad and the Pitomnik defence *Staffel* for the Channel front early in 1943. He was seriously injured in a forced landing at St Omer on 21 December 1943 and, after recovery, would spend the rest of the war as a fighter instructor.

In relaxed mood, Oberfeldwebel Wilhelm Freuwörth wears the Knight's Cross awarded to him in the immediate aftermath of Stalingrad when a member of 2./JG 52. He was one of many Russian front *Experten* subsequently posted to the west (where this photograph was taken). After being severely injured when his machine somersaulted on landing late in 1943, he spent the remaining months of the war with training units

December's three other casualties were all suffered in the east. Having claimed his half-century on 27 September, Leutnant Johannes Bunzek of III./JG 52 had increased his tally to 75 before being reported missing in action after a dogfight west of Nikopol on 11 December. Lost on that same day, and reportedly in similar circumstances, near Zhitomir was 12./JG 51's Leutnant Rudolf Wagner. He had joined IV./JG 51 the previous year, and it must therefore be assumed that a good proportion of his 81 victories may well have been scored on Fw 190s, but the *Gruppe* had long been re-established on *Gustavs* by the time he went missing.

Last, and highest ranking, of the year's losses was Major Hubertus von Bonin, the *Geschwaderkommodore* of JG 54. His operational career had begun with the *Legion Condor* in Spain, where he claimed four Republican fighters during the winter of 1938-39. He was credited with his first nine World War 2 victories in 1940 while *Gruppenkommandeur* of I./JG 54. After then being appointed *Kommandeur* of III./JG 52 on the Russian front – with whom he amassed 55 of his 64 Soviet kills – von Bonin returned to JG 54 to take the place of the departing Oberstleutnant Hannes Trautloft as *Kommodore* early in July 1943. He was killed in action near Orsha on 15 December.

The awards announced in the last two months of 1943 hardly made up for this grim list of casualties. In fact, it was almost as if the pen-pushers back in Berlin were intent on tidying up the books for the year's end. Three of the five Knight's Crosses awarded during this time were posthumous, and a fourth went to a pilot (Werner Quast) who had already spent more than four months in Soviet captivity.

The only one of the five to receive the decoration in person, on 14 December, was Hauptmann Maximilian Mayerl. He had opened his Russian front score sheet with a brace of Pe-2s five weeks into *Barbarossa*.

But even he had been withdrawn from frontline operations just six days prior to his award, having relinquished command of 9./JG 51 to take up the first of a succession of training appointments.

By the close of 1943 the air war in the east was very different to what it had been two-and-a-half years earlier. The opening days of 'clay pigeon campaigning' had long gone, as too were many of the *Experten* who had boosted their scores at the expense of the hapless and ill-prepared Russian fighter pilots and bomber crews in that summer of 1941. Now the enemy was better trained, was employing better tactics and was flying better aircraft – the latter in ever growing, and soon to be overwhelming numbers.

The *Jagdwaffe* was also changing. Greatly reduced in strength by the transfer away of units to shore up other fronts, more and more of its members were youngsters newly arrived from fighter schools in Germany and occupied western Europe. And it was these *Nachwuchs*, or 'second-generation', pilots who would have to face the revitalised Red Air Force during the remaining months of the war.

Large numbers of them would perish in the bitter fighting that lay ahead, but others rose to the challenge, equalling – and in some cases surpassing – the achievements of their experienced predecessors. The prime example, of course, is Erich Hartmann, who did not arrive at the front until late 1942, but who ended the war with a staggering 352 victories as the highest scoring fighter pilot in history.

Many more, although less spectacularly successful (and certainly less well known), would join the ranks of the Russian front's semi-centurions. One such was 20-year-old Heinz 'Esau' Ewald – no relation to Major Wolfgang Ewald now in a Soviet PoW camp – whose first victory (a Yak fighter downed in a head-on confrontation) had been a matter more of luck than judgement. Once back at base, this kill earned the impetuous young unteroffizier 15 push-ups from his veteran flight leader Feldwebel Hans Ellendt, himself already well on the way to his half-century. The latter also gave Ewald some pithy words of advice to the effect that 'anybody who tackles Ivan snout to snout, and is then fool enough to open fire into the bargain, isn't going to be around for long!'

Heinz Ewald took good heed. So much so that on the last day of 1943 he enjoyed what he would later describe as 'my most successful sortie – three kills in 18 minutes!'

Ewald's unit, II./JG 52, was at that time based at Bagerovo, in the eastern Crimea, and had just returned from escorting a raid by He 111 bombers on the bridgehead recently established on the peninsula by Soviet forces, when suddenly the order was given to scramble again. A formation of *Shturmoviks* was approaching the field;

'As my machine is unserviceable, I run across to the '109 assigned to the *Gruppen-Adjutant*, Leutnant Will van de Kamp, which he rarely flies. Seeing my intentions, the mechanics dash after me. As I take possession, i.e. climb into the cockpit, they are already busy with the starting handle. Quickly, fasten harness, lock canopy, ignition to M1 and M2, pull the starter – the DB 605's 1400 horses begin to howl – throttle gently forwards, the machine begins to move, full power and I head straight out across the field at right angles to the strip. She picks up more and more speed, dances a little, lifts off, floats as I deliberately hold her down, then retract undercarriage and full steam ahead, still at low level and with course due west.

'During my take-off, the Il-2s have been making their attacking run across the base – thank God, some way above me and diagonal to my line of flight, while their escorting fighters circle like vultures overhead. Although it's been firing wildly throughout, the field's flak hasn't hit a single one of the Russians. But our standing patrol, the only two of our fighters in the air, gets one of the escorting Yaks.

'By now I've turned about and am racing back across the field at 200 metres after the Il-2s. As I do so, I spot the Yak pilot's parachute drifting earthwards with another machine circling it. As I approach, this second Yak breaks off and chases after the retreating formation back towards the Russian lines. I quickly overhaul him, and a full burst from all barrels of my fighter envelop him from wingtip to wingtip. Debris and wreckage fly through the air. One large piece whizzes past dangerously just a hair's breadth above my cockpit. The rest, a ball of flame with a tail sticking out of it, smashes into the ground behind one of our flak emplacements. Hell's bells. "'*Radetzki 2*' – a kill!"

'But with such a head of steam on, and still flying east, I realise that I am rapidly closing on a *Schwarm* of Airacobras. I've got to lose speed fast, otherwise I'll overshoot the Cobras, find myself ahead of them and be a sitting duck. I wrench back on the throttle, open the radiator flaps and tramp alternately on the rudder pedals. Bravo, it's done the trick. I slow down and, much to my relief, the Ivans haven't spotted me – wrong!

'The Russian *Schwarmführer*, flying on the far left of the formation, unexpectedly makes a diving turn. It's a manoeuvre straight out of the textbook, but he shouldn't have done it, for I react to it in a split second,

One of the best and most successful of the younger generation of pilots during the latter part of the air war in the east, Leutnant Heinz Ewald of JG 52 poses in front of a late-model Bf 109G-6 bearing his own personal motif – the combination of 'E' and 'sow' that formed his nickname 'Esau'

almost instinctively, following him down and giving him plenty of lead before once again letting fly with all barrels. The result is that the Cobra flies straight through my hail of fire and never comes out of his diving turn. It steepens and he bores into the frozen Russian earth 300 metres away from the Yak. "'*Radetzki 2*' – a kill!"

'Then I hear a warning shout over the R/T – *"Achtung,* Esau!" But I've already caught a packet from one of the other Ivans. My machine has 28 bullet holes in it – the mechanic counted them after I landed. But I've not been touched and the crate is still perfectly flyable, although it takes a long while for the adjutant to get over what I've done to his bird!

'I am able to escape from my pursuer in a tight spiral. The whole affair isn't over yet though, for a couple of Yaks, probably detailed to cover the Russian formation's withdrawal, are still circling in the vicinity of our field. They are somewhat higher than me, but it's a bit of a cheek all the same, and they're probably looking for trouble. Still fired up with the fever of the chase, I first fly off eastwards and begin to climb. Then I reverse course and bore in to attack the two Yaks.

'I send three short bursts between the enemy fighters. I don't score any hits, but my fire forces them to turn, not in unison, but away from each other. Hurrah, now things look a lot better. I reef my fighter around so sharply that a black veil comes down momentarily in front of my eyes. Then I'm fully involved in a dogfight with one of the Yaks, while the other makes off.

'I follow the Yak around in circle after circle. "There's plenty of time", I think to myself. Now I hear the deep, unmistakeable tones of my *Kommandeur*, Hauptmann Barkhorn, in my earphones – "Keep it up, '*Radetzki 2*', and then give him a full deflection burst!" "Victor – Victor". We're still going round like a carousel. I can see my opponent clearly in his cockpit. This Russian is not just a good pilot, he's getting every ounce he can out of his fighter. Very slowly I edge into position to open fire.

'The end, when it comes, is very quick. Suddenly, the Yak pulls out of its turn and does a flick half roll. I am a hundredth of a second behind him, but now the advantage is with me. He makes a shallow curve to the east. A well-aimed salvo hits the fleeing Yak fair and square. The Russian machine rears up, then trundles over into a dive, trailing smoke and shedding pieces. Just above the round it levels out and now the right undercarriage leg comes down. The wheel clips the top of a small hill and the Yak slides along the ground for a good 60 metres, burning as it goes. "'*Radetzki 2*', reporting third kill!"'

Although 1944 has been described by one campaign historian as 'beginning fairly quietly', the members of JG 51 may not have agreed. For it was they who suffered all four of the Russian front semi-centurion casualties sustained during the first two months of the year.

9. *Staffel's* Unteroffizier Gabriel Tautscher fell victim to Soviet flak on 12 January when his score was standing at 55. Ten days later Oberfeldwebel Otto Gaiser, a 74-victory *Experte* of 10./JG 51, was reported missing – possibly also brought down by enemy ground fire. The *Staffel* diary notes;

'Oberfeldwebel Otto Gaiser took off in "White 11" at 1025 hrs on a *freie Jagd* sortie. At 1045 hrs he reported encountering four Il-2s at 200 metres east of Lubyan. Since then he has been missing.

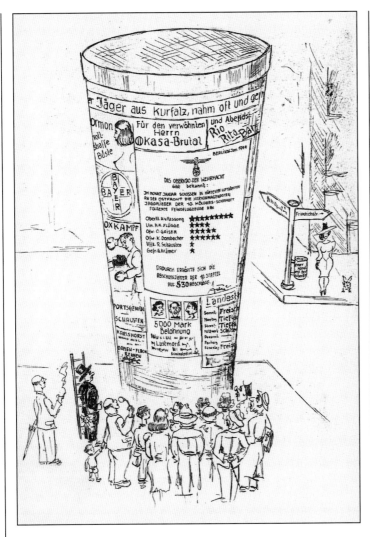

An example of the many humorous illustrations contained in 10./JG 51's unofficial unit diary, this one has a unique way of recording its successes of January 1944. On a typical Berlin street corner advertising column, amid a jumble of ads for such delights as bust-enhancing cream, a boxing match, virility pills, evenings at the Rio Rita Bar, a women's athletics meeting and the offer of a 5000-Mark reward for help in tracking down a sex murderer, there is a large poster headed, 'The *Oberkommando der Wehrmacht* announces – In the month of January, in fierce aerial fighting on the eastern front, the leading pilots of the 10th Mölders mob shot down the following enemy aircraft'. And in the list below are the names of three semi-centurions – Oberleutnant Horst von Fassong leads with ten stars, Oberfeldwebel Otto Gaiser has five and Oberfeldwebel Kurt Dombacher six. Incidentally, the top-hatted chimney sweep with ladder at bottom left has nothing to do with 1./JG 54 – see the photograph of 'Toni' Döbele on page 49. Such a figure is a traditional symbol of good luck for the New Year in Germany

Otto Würfel of 8./JG 51, pictured here as an unteroffizier, was both promoted to leutnant and awarded the Knight's Cross while in Soviet captivity

'As aircraft searching for Oberfeldwebel Gaiser reported heavy ground fire in the area, we assume that the machine was damaged by flak and forced to land behind enemy lines. We do not give up hope of seeing our Otto again.'

But it was to be a vain hope. Gaiser had disappeared without trace. He had been recommended for the Knight's Cross (and promotion to leutnant) prior to his loss, and would be honoured with the award posthumously on 9 June 1944.

February's two casualties were the result of a mid-air collision between two oberfeldwebeln over Russian-held Rogatchev on 23rd of the month when Heinrich Dittlmann's machine had rammed that of Otto Würfel. One parachute was seen. It was Otto Würfel, whose 79 victories would earn him the Knight's Cross (announced on 4 May 1944, seven months before he died in a Soviet PoW camp). Heinrich Dittlmann's final total of 57 went unrecognised.

Of the above quartet, only Otto Gaiser was flying a *Gustav* at the time of his loss. The other three, all from III./JG 51, were piloting Fw 190s, and it is therefore probable that most, if indeed not *all*, of the totals credited to them were achieved on Focke-Wulfs. But as it is not possible to state this with certainty, their names have been included here (and in the appendix) for the record.

February 1944 also saw six new Knight's Cross recipients – plus one posthumous award – for scores ranging from 36 to 85. The latter had been amassed by Leutnant Gerhard Loos of JG 54. He was another whose victories had been claimed on both Bf 109s and Fw 190s. By the time of his decoration, he was already serving as the *Staffelkapitän* of 8./JG 54 in Defence of the Reich. Loos would be lost in action there the following month after having added a further 14 kills to his reported Russian front total of 78.

The seemingly anomalous award of the Knight's Cross this late in the war for 'just' 36 enemy aircraft destroyed was a special case, for Hauptmann Herbert Findeisen was a reconnaissance pilot! In fact, he came very close to becoming the Luftwaffe's only reconnaissance semi-centurion. His score was standing at 42 when he eventually exchanged the Bf 109s of 2./NAGr 4 for the Fw 190s of JG 54 late in 1944. Findeisen ended the war as the *Kommandeur* of II./JG 54 with a final total of 67.

Over the next three months – March to May 1944, during which time the Red Army drove the German troops out of the southern Ukraine and began to prepare for its greatest offensive of all, on the central sector – awards and losses among the Luftwaffe's semi-centurions were almost equal. But it is the detail behind this bald fact that reveals the true state of affairs on the Russian front at this period.

Of the 12 Knight's Crosses announced, five went to pilots already either dead or in enemy captivity. And the single set of Oak Leaves, presented to Major Reinhard Seiler on 2 March, were for the century he had reached on the second day of *Zitadelle* back in July 1943 when he

Major Reinhard Seiler, *Gruppen-kommandeur* of III./JG 54 (a post he held from October 1941 until mid-April 1943), is greeted by his dog soon after returning from a mission. Assuming command of I. *Gruppe* in the spring of 1943, Seiler was severely wounded on the second day of Operation *Zitadelle*. Retired from operations, he ended the war as *Kommodore* of training Geschwader JG 104

himself was forced to bale out severely wounded. He had not flown operationally since.

More tellingly perhaps, only three of the 14 casualties suffered during this same time actually fell on the main Russian fronts. The others had all claimed their 50+ victories against the Soviets and – apart from Albert Brunner up in the Arctic – had already been posted to other theatres.

The first of the trio to be lost was Feldwebel Helmut Holtz of 11./JG 51, who had achieved 56 kills against the Red Air Force before his own *Gustav*, 'Black 14', went down in the fierce fighting around Tarnopol on 18 April. Less than a month later, on 15 May, 10./JG 51's Leutnant Herbert Friebel lost his life in the same area of southeastern Poland. The *Staffel* diary records;

'Leutnant Friebel came to us from 12. *Staffel*, not having flown for a long time because of an earlier wound. He took over leadership of the *Staffel* on 1 May 1944. On 15 May 1944 he flew his first mission with us, during which he shot down a Yak-9 southwest of Tarnopol. That afternoon he took off again to lead a *Schwarm* on a *freie Jagd* sweep. He became involved in a dogfight with ten La-5s. At an altitude of 1000 metres he tried to follow an enemy machine through a diving turn. This resulted in his hitting the ground behind the frontlines southwest of Tarnopol, three kilometres to the west of Viykizhimka. His machine burst into flames on impact and was totally destroyed.

'Leutnant Friebel had 58 victories and had been decorated with the Knight's Cross (on 24 January 1943 for his then 51 kills).'

The area where both Holtz and Friebel were lost reveals just how far JG 51 had been forced to retreat on the central sector. The *Geschwader*, which had once stood at the very gates of Moscow, was now fighting along the Polish border. Similarly, in the south, JG 52, which little more than a year earlier had still been operating down deep in the Caucasus, had since been pushed off the Crimea and driven out of the Ukraine altogether, and was now back in Rumania – its original jumping-off point for *Barbarossa*.

And it was over Rumania that another veteran NCO semi-centurion was lost on the last day of May 1944. Feldwebel Karl Schumacher of III./JG 52 had also only recently recovered from severe wounds – inflicted during the opening hours of *Zitadelle* – and had returned to operations to raise his final total to 56, before being shot down near Jassy. A fellow feldwebel reported that Schumacher managed to bale out, but that his parachute failed to open.

All the other fatalities during the spring of 1944, including Oak Leaves wearers Oberstleutnant Friedrich-Karl Müller, Major Kurt Ubben and Oberleutnant Otto Wessling, had been suffered over the Reich or pre-invasion France – except one. And this single exception provided yet further proof of just how tightly the net was closing in on Germany.

Since being withdrawn from the Russian front late in 1942 for service in North Africa, JG 77 had continued to operate in the Mediterranean. Then, in October 1943, III./JG 77 was transferred to Mizil, in Rumania, where that country's vital oilfields were now being threatened not only by the Soviets advancing from the east, but also by attack from the southwest by American heavy bombers of the Fifteenth Air Force flying up from bases recently established in Italy.

Portrayed in pre-Knight's Cross mode, Oberfeldwebel Otto Wessling wears around his neck instead a scarf decorated with the 'Seahorse' emblem of 9./JG 3. After claiming 62 Russian front kills, the now Leutnant Wessling joined IV./JG 3 in mid-1943, serving first in the Mediterranean and then the Reich. His final overall total of 83 before being killed by P-51s on 19 April 1944 earned him posthumous Oak Leaves three months later

Seated on the wheel of his *Emil* during the Balkan/Cretan campaign of spring 1941 (where he gained his first three victories, and established a reputation as a fighter-bomber specialist), Leutnant Emil Omert had risen to the rank of hauptmann, and command of III./JG 77, by the time he lost his life in action against US heavy bombers over Rumania on 24 April 1944. Both Otto Wessling and Emil Omert were allegedly shot by US fighter pilots, the former being strafed on the ground after surviving a forced landing southeast of Kassel, and the latter while descending by parachute near Ploesti

It was the latter, in the form of a raid by a mixed force of B-17s and B-24s on the marshalling yards at Ploesti on 24 April 1944, that had resulted in the loss of III./JG 77's *Gruppenkommandeur*, and ex-Russian front semi-centurion, Hauptmann Emil Omert. He had led his *Gustavs* in a frontal attack on the estimated 500-strong stream of enemy bombers. One of the pilots behind him described what it was like;

'We attack the bombers head-on, like infantry storming an enemy position. When I open fire with my own cannon, the whole machine shakes. The large silver birds glittering in the sun make an imposing picture – simply horribly beautiful.'

After the first firing pass, the pilots waited for further orders from their *Kommandeur* over the R/T. But none were forthcoming. Hauptmann Omert's 'Yellow 1' had already gone down. He had succeeded in baling out, but was reportedly shot in his parachute by one of the bombers' strong force of escorting fighters.

The Red Army's great central sector summer offensive of 1944, launched on 22 June to coincide with the third anniversary of *Barbarossa*, dwarfed everything that had gone before. By the time it ended in August, all Soviet territory still in German hands had been retaken, as had most of the Baltic States. Russian troops were poised in front of Warsaw and along the borders of East Prussia, waiting for the spring to deliver the final blow. Hitler had lost 28 of his 34 divisions and over 300,000 men – more than were sacrificed at Stalingrad – in his futile effort to stem the seemingly unstoppable Red tide.

Against this backdrop of massive losses on the ground, those in the air – at least as far as the semi-centurions were concerned – would prove to be remarkably light. On 19 June, just 72 hours before the central front offensive began, 4./JG 54's Leutnant Helmut Grollmus had been

brought down by enemy flak east of Viipuri during II./JG 54's second brief deployment on (southern) Finnish soil.

The 75-victory Grollmus had of course been flying a Focke-Wulf ('White 11') at the time of his loss – all three of JG 54's *Gruppen* in the east had long been equipped with Fw 190s. But Grollmus' operational career with II./JG 54 had begun as an unteroffizier back in early 1942, and all his initial successes had been scored on Bf 109s.

Only one 50+ *Experte* was to be lost on the central sector during the entire ten weeks of the Soviet summer offensive. This was Hauptmann Edwin Thiel, who had only recently assumed command of JG 51's Fw 190-equipped *Stabsstaffel*. During a low-level attack on enemy forces near Kobryn on 14 July, Thiel's Focke-Wulf took a direct flak hit on the right wing. It immediately flipped over onto its left and plunged the 200 metres into a thick wood below, killing the pilot instantly.

Thiel had been flying on operations even longer than Helmut Grollmus, serving with JG 52 at the beginning of the war, before

A *Rotte* (two-aircraft formation) of Bf 109G-6s of 8./JG 51 taxi out for their next mission on the central sector shortly before the launch of the Red Army's major summer offensive of 1944

The only semi-centurion to be lost during the Soviet summer offensive (shot down by enemy flak east of Brest-Litovsk on 14 July 1944), Edwin Thiel had been presented with his Knight's Cross on 16 April 1943 when an oberleutnant and *Staffelkapitän* of 2./JG 51

transferring to JG 51, where he had replaced the fallen Erwin Fleig as *Kapitän* of 2. *Staffel* in May 1942. All his earlier kills had also thus been achieved on Messerschmitts. Having been awarded the Knight's Cross on 16 April 1943 (for his then total of 51 victories), Hauptmann Edwin Thiel's final Russian front score was 76.

Another indication of Hitler's near paranoid obsession with the threat posed by the western allies was that, with the Red Army almost on his eastern doorstep, the three understrength *Jagdgeschwader* standing in its path were left to their own devices all but unaided, whereas the invasion of Normandy had already seen practically the entire day fighter strength of the Defence of the Reich organisation rushed post-haste to France. This was to have a devastating effect on the *Jagdwaffe*, and included the loss of four ex-Russian front 50+ *Experten* between June and August.

Oberleutnant Eugen-Ludwig Zweigart, the *Staffelkapitän* of 8./JG 54, was shot down by Mustangs on D-Day+2 (8 June 1944). Fellow *Kapitän* Leutnant Horst Forbrig of 2. *Staffel* was killed in action over Caen four days later. Their final overall totals were 69 and 58 respectively. Doubt surrounds the exact score achieved by III./JG 52's long-serving Leutnant Friedrich Wachowiak before his transfer to the invasion front and loss to Spitfires on 16 July. Some sources refer to his having claimed 'at least 86' Soviet victims. Others maintain a truer figure would be over 120 – perhaps even as many as 140. As he had been nominated for the Oak Leaves prior to his death, the latter estimates may be nearer the mark.

Last of the four was Oberleutnant Kurt Ebener, now the *Staffelkapitän* of 5./JG 11, who was forced to bale out of his badly damaged *Gustav* after tangling with US fighters southeast of Paris on 23 August and parachuted severely wounded into Allied captivity. It is on record that all but five of his final total of 57 were claimed in the east as a member of JG 3 – among them the 33 that had made him the highest scorer of Stalingrad's Pitomnik defence *Staffel*.

Meanwhile, what of JG 52 down in Rumania and southern Poland throughout these same summer months? Among their semi-centurions, there had been one new Knight's Cross recipient and casualty . . . and both were the same man. Back in March 1944, the then Feldwebel Herbert Bachnick had enjoyed a run of successes during III./JG 52's 12-day stay at Proskurov, in the western Ukraine. Of the *Gruppe's* collective total of 46 during this period, he alone had been respon sible for 21 of them. Bachnick claimed four victories on one day and five more on each of two other days. Among them was his 75th, which he had claimed on 14 March.

On 27 July 1944, since promoted to leutnant and with his score standing at 79, Herbert Bachnick was awarded the Knight's Cross. His 80th, and last, went down on 7 August when III./JG 52 engaged a force of Fifteenth Air Force heavy

Oberleutnant Eugen-Ludwig Zweigart, 50+ Russian front *Experte* and *Staffelkapitän* of 8./JG 54, was shot down over Normandy on D-Day+2 (8 June 1944)

bombers attacking synthetic-oil refineries at Blechhammer, in Upper Silesia. Bachnick's own *Gustav* was severely damaged in the action, and he tried to put it down in a forced landing. But with the controls all but useless, he was unable to avoid a railway embankment in his path and lost his life in the resulting crash.

JG 52's withdrawal into Rumania had meant that it too was now within the range of US four-engined bombers flying up from Italy. The *Geschwader* had soon found itself embroiled in a two-front war. Although its paramount task remained that of protecting its own ground troops from attack by low-flying Soviet aircraft in the east, it would henceforth be called upon with increasing frequency to combat the high-altitude raids by American bombers on targets in its rear.

Such missions against the Fifteenth Air Force's 'heavies' were known to the Luftwaffe as *Sternflüge*, or 'starflights', and the combination of having to operate at low-level over the Russian frontlines one day, and then be ordered up against a high-flying stream of heavily escorted four-engined bombers the next, placed an enormous strain on the pilots of JG 52.

Heinz 'Esau' Ewald, by now one of the more experienced members of the *Geschwader*, has left a vivid description of what it was like;

'Our *Gruppe* (II./JG 52) is based at Husi, on the west bank of the Pruth just inside the Rumanian border. We are flying several missions almost every day against the east, supporting Oberstleutnant Rudel's SG 2. I often have to escort him when he goes hunting Russian tanks along the front line in his special tank-busting machine – a Ju 87 equipped with two underwing 3.7 cm cannon.

'But on this morning of 24 June 1944 we receive an order by radio – "Assemble for starflight!" We, that is about 60-70 German fighters based in southeast Europe, then gather on three fields well behind the front in central Rumania in readiness to tackle more than 200 four-engined bombers and more than 100 escorting fighters. So, exactly as we have practised three times already, after assembly we set out from Buzow against the US bomber stream.

'We climb to a height of 7300 metres. Far off, we can see Rumania's largest oil refinery already nicely blanketed in a layer of artificial fog. This is again today's target for the US attackers flying in from Italy – then over the R/T – "To all 'Knights' (us) from 'Barbarossa' (ground control), many 'furniture vans' (heavy bombers) and 'indians' (enemy fighters) reported in grid sector 'QSÜ Caruso North'!"

'But we've already spotted them – box after box of tiny silver dashes on the horizon. For us Russian front fighter pilots, this picture of the enemy's overwhelming superiority brings our hearts into our mouths. "That's an awful lot of USA tin heading our way!" someone says in my headphones. Then the voice of the *Staffelkapitän* – "Achtung, all little brothers. 'Indians' sitting behind the third box!" Although it's more than a little cold up here at 7000 metres, even in June, I can feel the sweat trickling into my oxygen mask.

'We are flying in what we call "Nuremberg rally parade" formation – six abreast. Unfortunately, today there are only 27 of us due to serviceability problems. The wall of heavily armed silver shapes is getting ever closer, for we have cut across their course slightly in order to carry out our first attack before the enemy reaches the Ploesti target area. And we succeed, making our initial pass head-on before the first box of 45 bombers alters course to start its bomb run.

'Bent low over the control column, we race towards the wall of steel. I clench my teeth and my 21-year-old heart is pounding like a trip-hammer. A thick curtain of fiery pearl beads some 80 metres wide comes rushing towards us. A good thing it's directed against – and divided between – all of us. Individually, we'd be chopped up into little slices.

'My bomber, a Liberator, grows ever bigger in my gunsight until, suddenly, it's enormous! "Now Esau, open fire – just like your first kill, snout to snout". I let fly! Jagged fountains erupt all over the bomber as my shells and bullets gnaw hungrily at splintering glass, through tanks containing thousands of litres of fuel and into its metal body and wings – about six seconds of iron music, and then I pull up and away damned close above the Liberator.

'Now the dense web of tracer chases after us, the explosive rounds bursting like deadly fireworks. Good that we can't hear the staccato bellowing of the American weapons. After our first pass, two bombers have already been blasted out of the box and are heading down towards mother earth in ever tighter spirals. Three others are smoking badly – among them my bomber, the second on the right. But boy, can these monsters absorb a lot of iron and steel!

'Now the escorting fighters are diving down towards us, for we have already reversed course and are preparing to attack the same box from the rear. What happens next is first rate. The American fighters turn away and leave us alone. They don't want to get hit by the fire being hosed about all over the sky by their own bombers. It now becomes clear that our machines are much too slow for a stern chase. The individual duels between us and the bombers' tail and fuselage gunners last much too long.

'My bomber must have been damaged more seriously during my frontal pass than I first thought, for it has dropped out of formation slightly and is lagging behind. I give it another long salvo with everything I've got. A chain of hits marches across its left-hand engines. After a small explosion in the port inner, the huge crate drops away from the box in a shallow curve with its entire left wing in flames.

'The *Staffelkapitän* again – "All little brothers close up, stick together, get back in formation! Get in tight! Victor! Victor!" We attack the same box for a third time. Unfortunately we are no longer 27 little brothers. Several have reported damage to their machines. Three have been wounded. From others – just silence.

'We – that is, the remains of the *Gruppe* – become completely scattered after our third and final pass. The bombers' escorting Mustangs dive down firing wildly. Now things really get hot as dogfights break out all over the place. My wingman and I are far out to the right, so these "boys" are not yet a danger to us. But we have strayed too close to the next box of bombers and so get a large dose of lead from their gunners instead.

'We are already a good 300 metres off to the flank of the last box when there is a tremendous bang. Thin smoke immediately fills the cockpit and, shortly afterwards, tongues of flame being to lick out from under the instrument panel. I can feel the heat on my lower legs. "Esau, you've got to get out of here!" I pull the canopy emergency jettison lever, but the canopy refuses to budge. By now the smoke is much thicker, and it's

stinging my eyes. Luckily I can still breathe – my oxygen mask fits tightly
and the regulator is working properly.

'But I have to do something fast. I unlock the canopy, just as I would
after any normal landing, and then raise both hands above my head and
push hard against the glass of the cockpit roof. It is said that people in
mortal danger are often able to summon up superhuman strength. I must
have been blessed with something similar, for I actually manage to lift the
canopy up about two centimetres.

'There is a whistling noise – and then the canopy is gone. I find myself
in a gentle turn, but the flames from the engine compartment are
now much fiercer. I unfasten my harness and hurl myself out in one
movement. My neck receives a terrible wrench. I have forgotten to
disconnect my "pigtail" – the cord of my throat mike. Then, at last, I am
free of my doomed fighter.

'I let myself plummet through space, tumbling over and over, as I don't
want to be shot in my parachute by the escorting American fighters as
Hannes Blätter from Bremen was yesterday. Throughout our whole time
on the southeastern front, Russian pilots have never shot at German pilots
in their parachutes. Perhaps the Americans are practising "total war"!

'At a height of about 1000 metres I pull the parachute release. For a
few interminable seconds absolutely nothing happens. Then the canopy
opens with such a jolt I feel as if I am being stretched on the rack. At first,
after my wild head over heels descent, I get the impression that the
parachute is actually lifting me upwards, but then I realise I am slowly
floating down at about five metres a second.

'From a few thousand metres above comes the monotonous drone of
the heavy bombers, the hammering of their on-board weapons and the
deeper thump of our own cannon. I can see the spot where I'll be coming
down – a small patch of forest not far from a village. It's now that I hear
a huge explosion as, off to one side behind me, a Liberator with its full
bomb load and about 5000 litres of fuel still in its tanks hits the ground.
There are four large mushrooms of smoke in the sky above me, a couple
of them still raining debris. Then there's no time to see more.

'With my hands in front of my eyes and legs pressed tightly together,
I crash into the topmost branches of an 8-12 metre high stand of mixed
trees. I take several of the branches with me, but they help to break my fall
and I come to earth gently enough. My left ankle, however, feels as if it has
a thousand needles sticking in it. And when I get to my feet I discover that
both my shoes are full of blood.'

What Heinz Ewald fails to mention is just how badly injured he really
was. Of the ten *Gustavs* of 6./JG 52 that had taken off on that day's
starflight, only two returned to base – those of the *Staffelkapitän* and his
wingman. The former counted the cost;

'Two aircraft were damaged and had to make emergency landings,
another came down on an enemy occupied airfield and five of our pilots
were shot down. Of these, two were killed instantly and three parachuted.
Only one landed safely, for one was machine-gunned by the Mustangs
during his descent (this was, in fact, the unfortunate Unteroffizier Blätter
referred to mistakenly in the account above), and Leutnant Ewald baled
out of his burning machine at the last moment, having suffered such
severe burns that his recovery was in doubt for a very long time.'

Hauptmann Alfred Teumer was one of two ex-Russian front semi-centurions to be lost in the west during the last quarter of 1944 flying the Me 262. Seen here as a leutnant with JG 54 in Russia with a pair of four-legged companions (an Airedale terrier and a fox cub), Teumer was killed on 1 October 1944

Twenty-four hours later, the survivors of II./JG 52 were back in action against their traditional foe, the Red Air Force. And so it would continue for the remainder of the year, with the Russian front Bf 109 *Gruppen* – principally those of JGs 51 and 52 – remaining very much the underdogs, both in terms of the numbers of Russian aircraft opposing them and also, or so it would seem, in the eyes of the planners in Berlin, whose attention was still firmly fixed on operations in the west and over the Reich itself.

It is again indicative that not one 50+ *Experte* was killed in action against the Soviets during the last three months of 1944, whereas four ex-Russian front semi-centurions lost their lives over Germany's western provinces during this period. The first was the result of an accident. Alfred Teumer had joined JG 54 as a feldwebel back in December 1941. In the next two-and-a-half years he was to be credited with 66 Russian aircraft destroyed before being transferred to Defence of the Reich duties in May 1944.

Then, on 1 October 1944, Teumer was posted to the Me 262-equipped *Erprobungskommando* Nowotny, only to be killed three days later when his jet fighter suffered an engine flame-out when coming in to land at Hesepe.

The other three casualties were all suffered in December 1944 against the backcloth of the run-up to, or during the course of, Hitler's final gamble in the west – the ill-judged and disastrous counter-offensive in the Ardennes. Veteran NCO Alexander Preinfalk (who, incidentally, had been born at Baku, in the Caucasus – the ultimate oilfield goal of the abortive 1942 summer offensive) had claimed 59 Soviet victims while flying with JG 77 in the east between October 1941 and September 1942. Since transferred to JG 53 and Reich's Defence, he was shot down by P-47s northeast of Karlsruhe on 12 December.

Robert 'Bazi' Weiss' operational career had begun with JG 26 in 1941-42 on the Channel coast, where he was credited with three RAF Spitfires. He then joined I./JG 54 in Russia, claiming an estimated 90 Russian aircraft while flying both Bf 109s and Fw 190s. Having been appointed *Gruppenkommandeur* of III./JG 54 in the west on 21 July 1944, Hauptmann Weiss was leading elements of his unit on a hunt for Typhoon fighter-bombers of the RAF over the Dortmund-Ems canal

On the last day of 1944, Oberleutnant Hans Schleef – long-serving member of JG 3, but now *Staffelkapitän* of 16./JG 4 – was brought down by US Thunderbolts west of Mannheim. At the time of his loss, Schleef's overall total was just two (some sources say one) short of the century

area on 29 December when their Fw 190D-9s were bounced by Norwegian-flown Spitfires. Among the losses was the *Kommandeur* in his 'Black 10'. With a final overall total of 121, Robert Weiss would be honoured with posthumous Oak Leaves on 12 March 1945.

The last of the more than 30 semi-centurions to be killed or reported missing in 1944 – on the last day of the year – was Oberleutnant Hans Schleef. A long-serving member of JG 3, Schleef had achieved 92 Russian kills before he too was posted to Reich's Defence. As the *Staffelkapitän* of 16./JG 4, Schleef fell victim to American P-47s patrolling west of the Rhine.

Meanwhile, on the Russian front, those pilots and units that had *not* been pulled out of the line to serve in other theatres continued to do all they could to halt the inexorable advance of the Soviet war machine. And while their scores were not as astronomically high as they had been in the balmy days of *Barbarossa*, they were still exacting a considerable toll.

On 1 September 1944, for example, the 36th Russian aircraft claimed by future semi-centurion Feldwebel Adolf Nehrig gave JG 52 its 9999th kill of the war to date – the 10,000th would fall to Major Adolf Borchers 24 hours later (see *Osprey Aviation Elite Units 15 - Jagdgeschwader 52* for further details).

But not even the most successful *Jagdgeschwader* in the Luftwaffe could prevent the collapse of the southern sector, as first Rumania and then Bulgaria concluded separate treaties with the Soviet Union, before declaring war on their erstwhile German ally. The Rumanian declaration on 25 August had caught the Germans off-guard. The Wehrmacht staged a fighting withdrawal, but was unable to stop the Red Army from quickly overrunning the country. On 29 August the oil terminal at Constanza, which III./JG 52 had protected with such vigour over three years earlier, fell to a combined Soviet land and sea assault. The Ploesti oilfields were lost a day later, and on 31 August Russian troops marched into the Rumanian capital, Bucharest.

As the war progressed, the celebrations surrounding a pilot's reaching his half-century became less elaborate. No sign of floral garlands or bottles of champagne here for the latest addition to the ranks of the semi-centurions, who is being greeted by his chief mechanic – just a crude piece of cardboard hung round his neck, baldly proclaiming '50th'. Unfortunately, the original print of this photograph is not sharp enough to identify the pilot with any certainty, but it has been suggested that it could well be future 203-victory *Experte* Hauptmann Helmut Lipfert

The Bulgarians had tried a different ploy, announcing their 'retirement from the war' on 26 August. But their self-proclaimed state of neutrality availed them little. The Russians promptly invaded and occupied Bulgaria, which then perforce declared war on Germany on 8 September.

While the southern sector was rapidly coming apart at the seams, an uneasy lull had descended on the central front. After the effort they

had expended on their great summer offensive, Soviet forces were utilising the early autumn months to prepare for the coming battle of Germany. Still standing in their path in central Poland, the pilots of JG 51 were grateful for the respite – but were fully aware of the fact that it couldn't last long. 13. *Staffel's* unknown diarist caught the mood;

'6 October: Peace and quiet – before the storm? – sleep from morning till evening, a good meal and then off to the cinema – that's our daily work schedule. "Negus" (121-victory *Experte* Oberfeldwebel Heinz Marquardt) reckons the war will begin again in a day or two.

'7 October: Today began just like any other. Quiet all morning, but then at midday all hell breaks loose from every corner. The Russians are pushing hard, trying to enlarge their bridgehead. To support their ground troops they're sending over their cement-bombers (Il-2 *Shturmoviks*) and Bostons, and, best of all, with minimal fighter escort. The first *Schwarm* to scramble makes the most of it – nine victories, including three each for Leutnant Kalden and Oberfeldwebel Marquardt – but the next sortie is a complete dud, and it's all the fault of the ops room, for it's an absolute waste of time to give the order to scramble against Bostons that are already over the "*Gartenzaun*" ("garden fence", which was the Luftwaffe codename for a unit's own base).'

Leutnant Peter Kalden had been appointed *Kapitän* of 10./JG 51 on 17 July 1944 (the *Staffel* was redesignated 13./JG 51 the following month). The 19 Soviet aircraft he shot down during October, all to the north of Warsaw, raised his total to 64. This was apparently regarded by the unit at the time as the number required to win the Knight's Cross, as witness the following diary entry;

'24 October: Another *Dödel* (Knight's Cross) on the way to the 13th mob! Today, Leutnant Kalden got his 64th – the aim of every fighter pilot. When he landed, he was greeted with shouts and cheers as he was lifted out of the cockpit, and a large wooden *Dödel*, the size of a breast-plate, was hung around his neck.'

But Luftwaffe bureaucracy worked at a somewhat more leisurely pace than the *Staffel* carpenter. Leutnant Kalden's award was not announced until 6 December, and it would be another 11 days after that before Generalmajor Robert Fuchs, the divisional commander, actually arrived to present it. One other Knight's Cross had been awarded in the interim, however. Kalden's CO, Hauptmann Heinz Lange, the *Gruppenkommandeur* of IV./JG 51, had received his on 18 November for a total of 70 victories, all but one scored in the east.

Meanwhile, to the south, with Rumania and Bulgaria already securely in their hands, Soviet forces were now intent on taking Hungary. On 8 December they launched an offensive aimed at encircling and isolating the country's capital, Budapest. II./JG 52 was based just to the west of the

Despite the worsening war situation there was still time for humour, even on the darkest of days. Another cartoon from the now 13./JG 51's unofficial diarist, this drawing shows a *Gustav* straining every fibre to get aloft as a Red Air Force bomber races past overhead, its rear-gunner waving a cheeky goodbye. The tagline, 'Bugger! These Bostons are fast!'

city, and after it was cut off (on 26 December) it was tasked with protecting the He 111 bombers that were attempting to keep the German garrison supplied by air. At the time, Heinz Ewald was flying the *Gruppe's* only *Kanonenboot*, or 'gunboat' – a Bf 109G armed with two additional cannon in underwing gondolas;

'When the ferry pilot first flew it in to Budaörs, nobody else wanted anything to do with it, as it was a good 200 kilograms heavier than our normal machines and was still fitted with the old, framed type of cockpit canopy. But as soon as they saw the effect it had when I opened up with all five weapons and in a single pass blew a pair of Airacobras out of the sky in tiny pieces, everybody wanted one!'

In Poland, too, IV./JG 51 were also getting new aircraft;

'For the past few days we've been re-equipping with G-14s. Seven machines have already arrived. The ferry pilot who wanted to fly Pifke's old "White 6" out crashed on take-off. The clapped-out old bird probably couldn't bear to be parted from us!

'31 December: Today is New Year's Eve. We're all armed with champagne, wine and schnapps. In the hours up to midnight we drank punch so that we could fully appreciate the broadcast of the *Führer's* speech. But after that, thing's really got going. At about 0300 hrs we all trooped off to the post office, where Pifke demonstrated his mountaineering skills by climbing through an upstairs window and shooing an SS man out of a young lady's bed. Then we spent an hour sitting chatting to the postmaster, who was celebrating with the "merry widow" and another girl. Feldwebel Asbach-Hache produced a bottle of schnapps from his pocket to justify our inviting ourselves to the party.

'Afterwards, it was back to the orderly room, where we kept going until morning, when we accompanied the chief as he did the rounds distributing schnapps, sausages, bread and New Year's greetings to one and all. By about midday the festivities came to a close. But during the night some unknown perpetrators – we suspect members of the HQ staff – had completely wrecked the HQ officers' mess so that the entire staff had to eat their New Year's dinner from the only two plates that remained unbroken.'

There were no such celebrations – at least, not officially – for the pilots of the Reich's Defence *Jagdgruppen*. They were ordered to remain sober and turn in early on New Year's Eve in preparation for a major effort early the next morning. Operation *Bodenplatte*, the New Year's Day attack by Luftwaffe fighters on Allied tactical airfields in the Low Countries and France, was a costly failure. Losses in men and machines were prohibitive – 22 by now irreplaceable unit commanders failed to return from the ambitious undertaking – and all to little end. A number of ex-Russian front semi-centurions took part in the operation of 1 January 1945, but only one was lost.

Leutnant Horst-Günther von Fassong came to the Luftwaffe from the army. His first two kills (a brace of I-16s) had been claimed on 3 July 1941 as a member of I./JG 51. Appointed *Staffelkapitän* of 10./JG 51 in February 1943, von Fassong had been credited with 62 Soviet aircraft by the time of his transfer to Defence of the Reich in April 1944. There, as *Kapitän* of 7./JG 11, he quickly added a quartet of B-17s to his tally, before being made *Kommandeur* of III./JG 11 the following month.

Pictured at a misty Neuruppin, northwest of Berlin, late in 1944, the 'Ace of Hearts' badge on the cowlings of these Bf 109K-4s identify them as machines of JG 77 – one of the many *Jagdgeschwader* soon to be rushed to the Russian front

In contrast to the numerous units that had been withdrawn from the Russian front since the start of *Barbarossa* to shore up other theatres in the west, von Fassong's *Gruppe* was one of the very few to make the journey the other way – from west to east. And even this was just a temporary measure when, in June 1944, III./JG 11 was hastily despatched to a landing strip near Minsk in the very eye of the breaking storm of the great Soviet summer offensive. Needless to say, the *Gruppe's* ten-week stay in the east had not the slightest effect on the course of events on the ground. But it did enable von Fassong to claim nine more Red Air Force victims.

It would appear that he achieved no further successes between III./JG 11's return to the Reich early in September and his taking off to lead the *Gruppe* in the low-level attack on the Allied airfield at Asch, in Belgium, that was the *Gruppe's* assigned objective on New Year's Day 1945. Caught close to the ground in the target area by a pair of US Thunderbolts, von Fassong's Fw 190 went in from a height of only 20-30 metres, cart-wheeling in a ball of flames upon impact.

Although *Bodenplatte* is regarded by many as the final nail in the coffin of the Luftwaffe's daylight fighter force, it in fact recovered sufficiently to participate in one last major air battle in Defence of the Reich. But the action over central Germany on 14 January 1945 was yet another disaster (the day resulted in 139 pilot casualties, against *Bodenplatte's* 232).

It was at this late juncture that Hitler finally acknowledged the enormity of the danger closing in on him from the east. For while the US 1st and 3rd Armies were still a few thousand metres short of Germany's main western frontier fortifications – the *Westwall*, or 'Siegfried Line' – in the east, the Soviets had already burst out of their bridgehead south of Warsaw. Within days they would be rampaging through the Reich's unprotected eastern provinces of Silesia, Pomerania and East Prussia.

The fact that the Red Army was no longer some distant colossus deep inside Russia, but rather an avenging force that was even now bearing down on his own capital, Berlin, concentrated the *Führer's* mind wonderfully. He ordered that all available fighter forces be rushed eastwards immediately to help stem the Soviet flood. But the *Jagdwaffe* of January 1945 was just a pale shadow of its former self.

Apart from those few veterans who had survived the previous six months' bloodletting – over Normandy and the Ardennes, during

79

Bodenplatte, and in Defence of the Reich – most units were made up predominantly of undeniably keen, but criminally under-trained youngsters. Supplies of aviation fuel had reached crisis point. And the enemy enjoyed virtually total air supremacy.

Under such circumstances it is hardly surprising that the Luftwaffe's losses soared dramatically. Most of the casualties came from the ranks of the inexperienced younger pilots. But the type of missions now being demanded of the *Jagdgruppen* – either escorting near-suicidal low-level attacks by ground assault Fw 190s, or themselves ground-strafing Soviet troops and armour – meant that survival depended just as much on luck as it did experience. And, inevitably, yet more semi-centurions were to fall in the war's final months.

One such was Oberleutnant Heinrich Füllgrabe, who had won the Knight's Cross as an oberfeldwebel with 9./JG 52 (the *Experten-Staffel*) more than two years earlier. Since that time, he had served both as an instructor and in Defence of the Reich, before returning to the Russian front and his old unit as *Geschwader-Adjutant* of JG 52 in December 1944. On 30 January 1945, Füllgrabe's *Gustav* was hit while carrying out a low-level attack on Soviet tanks near Brieg, in Silesia. From an altitude of just 45 metres, it went down on fire behind enemy lines.

Meanwhile, some 400 kilometres to the south, II./JG 52, based since 18 January at Veszprem, in Hungary, was still occasionally tangling with Mediterranean-based P-51s, as the *Kapitän* of 6. *Staffel* later recorded;

'It was around this time that we began to clash with Mustangs again, although unfortunately such encounters seldom ended happily for us. On one such occasion Leutnant Ewald and his *Schwarm* sighted eight of these American fighters north of Lake Balaton. Ewald was still seriously teed off with the *Amis* (Yanks) for shooting at him in his parachute over Rumania, so he waded straight in without properly assessing the situation.

JG 3 was also sent back to the east for the final rounds of the air war against the Soviets. Here, engine maintenance is performed on a Bf 109G-14 of 7. *Staffel* at Garz, on the Baltic coast, in the early spring of 1945

'He managed to hit one of the Mustangs, which cleared off trailing a thick banner of smoke, but within minutes another 20 or 30 had appeared on the scene. The original eight had called up reinforcements! Ewald and his three Messerschmitts were outnumbered nearly ten to one. The other three were quickly shot down, and soon the whole pack was concentrating on Ewald, who defended himself as best as he could. By continually turning, twisting and loosing off the odd burst, he was able to work his way back towards the field.

Seen here as an oberfeldwebel, Heinrich Füllgrabe was one of the acknowledged *Experten* of JG 52's famous 9. *Staffel* on the Russian front before his transfer back to the Reich. He rejoined his old unit in the east as *Geschwader-Adjutant* at the end of 1944, only to be lost in a low-level attack on Soviet armour in Silesia on 30 January 1945

'As he approached, still with three Mustangs on his tail, he suddenly straightened out, roaring past the Bishop's Palace in Veszpren at ground level – two NCOs standing on an upper balcony of the palace swore they looked down at Ewald as he flashed past below them with his engine bellowing at full throttle – before gaining a little altitude prior to landing . . . and flying straight into a burst of fire from the field's own flak defences!'

Ewald himself takes up the story from here;

'I'd just pulled the machine up a fraction, ready to lower the wheels and come in hot and fast, when a stream of tracer hits me from off to one side below. The bird is instantly nose heavy, and clearly intent on digging itself a crater in the mother earth of Hungary. Control stick back into my stomach – nothing! – think, trim wheel to minus – quickly! The snout of the ailing Me lifts – 250 metres, emergency jettison handle, canopy away, undo harness and out over the left-hand sill.

'I tug at the parachute release. The canopy opens and I am hanging 150 metres up in the air safe and sound when, suddenly, "ping, ping, zish, zissh". I hear metal, in other words, bullets whistling past me! German infantry detraining at the station not far from the airfield have spotted me and are shooting at "the Russian coming down by parachute", as eyewitnesses subsequently tell me. Luckily their aim is off, and after a few more swings of the 'chute I reach earth safely – that is, I come down flat on my face in a frozen meadow some 300 metres away from the landing field.'

The *Staffelkapitän's* account closes by saying that Ewald later drove across to the flak gunners and told them in no uncertain terms exactly what he thought of them. Ewald begs to differ. He has it that he was driven to the gun emplacement by a fellow pilot who was so enraged at the incident that after hurling abuse at the hapless gunners, he followed it up with a live hand-grenade! The flak crew quickly disappeared into their foxholes and nobody was hurt, but it had the desired effect. The battery commander telephoned *Gruppe* HQ to apologise for shooting down one of its fighters, while at the same time requesting that its pilots refrain from tossing hand-grenades about, otherwise he really would have to take the matter up with *Fliegerkorps!*

THE FINAL WEEKS

The last ten weeks of the war witnessed a final flurry of awards and decorations – more, even, than were conferred in the first ten weeks of *Barbarossa*. The anomalies seem to have persisted to the very end, however, for the scores of the 14 new Knight's Cross recipients during this period ranged from the low fifties to well into the eighties.

Among the former was Leutnant Herbert Bareuther, who had claimed 44 victories with JG 51 before being appointed *Kapitän* of 14./JG 3 in April 1945. This *Staffel* was part of IV.(*Sturm*)/JG 3, which had been a cornerstone of the Reich's Defence organisation (see *Osprey Aviation Elite Units 20 - Luftwaffe Sturmgruppen* for further details), prior to its becoming one of the *Jagdgruppen* involved in Hitler's mass transfer of fighter units from west to east in the latter half of January 1945. While commanding 14./JG 3 on the Oder front, Bareuther was able to add 11 more Soviet kills to his tally, but specific details are obscure, as too is the exact date of his Knight's Cross.

Leutnant Alfred Rauch was also a long serving member of JG 51. He had joined the *Geschwader* as an NCO in June 1940, scoring his first victory (a Hurricane over the Thames Estuary) two months later during the Battle of Britain. Following a spell as an instructor, his second kill had been a Soviet 'I-18' fighter downed northeast of Orel on 4 October 1941. Rauch was awarded the Knight's Cross on 9 April 1945 for a score of 53. This relatively low figure may be explained by the fact that latterly he had been a member of JG 51's Fw 190-equipped *Stabsstaffel*, with whom he had proven himself successful as a fighter-bomber specialist.

At the other end of the scale score-wise is a more familiar name – Leutnant Heinz Ewald. 'Esau' had reached his half-century over Veszprem on

Still smiling – pilots of 11./JG 3 gather round one of their Bf 109Ks on the Oder front in March 1945. On the original print it is just possible to make out the name *Mary* or *Marga* below the cockpit . . . and could that be the young lady herself sitting in the machine and getting all the attention?

29 December 1944. By the time he received his Knight's Cross on 20 April 1945 he had added another 32 kills to this total.

But this brief overview of the Russian front's semi-centurions is perhaps best concluded by detailing the fates of those half-dozen or so pilots who had achieved 50+ victories against the Soviets – some early on in their varied and illustrious operational careers – only to be lost in the final two months of hostilities when the war itself was clearly and irrevocably lost.

A prime example is Oberstleutnant Erich Leie, who is best known for his time with the famous JG 2 'Richthofen' in the Battle of Britain and on the Channel coast, when he flew alongside the likes of the legendary Helmut Wick and Walter Oesau. It was while serving as *Geschwader-Adjutant* of JG 2 on the Channel front that Erich Leie had been awarded the Knight's Cross (on 1 August 1941 for his then 21 victories against the RAF). He was transferred to the east early in 1943, assuming command of I./JG 51 on 18 January. Leie remained at the head of the *Gruppe* for almost two years, and during this period he claimed 71 Soviet aircraft destroyed – many while flying the Fw 190.

On 29 December 1944, Oberstleutnant Leie was officially appointed *Geschwaderkommodore* of JG 77. In the event, he did not actually take command until mid-January 1945, by which time JG 77 was another of the Reich's Defence *Geschwader* under orders to move with all speed to the Russian front. During the next seven weeks in Silesia, Erich Leie downed four more Red Air Force machines (the last two a pair of fighters on 7 March).

Fahnenjunker-Oberfeldwebel (Senior NCO Officer-Candidate) Alfred Rauch of JG 51's *Stabsstaffel* portrayed wearing the Knight's Cross awarded to him on 9 April 1945 – prior to his promotion to leutnant in the final month of the war in Europe

A veteran of both the Battle of Britain (with JG 2 'Richthofen', as seen here) and the Russian front (with JG 51 'Mölders'), Oberstleutnant Erich Leie, recently appointed *Geschwaderkommodore* of JG 77, was lost in action against Yak-9s over Silesia on 7 March 1945

On that date he led a reinforced *Schwarm* of six *Gustavs* in an emergency scramble against a reported incursion by a formation of Il-2s in the Schwarzwasser area. After claiming one of the Ilyushins' escorting

La-5s, Leie remained on patrol. Half-an-hour later, he sighted a gaggle of Yak-9s west of Bielitz. Again he picked off one of the Russian fighters from behind, but this time he had misjudged his speed and was unable to avoid crashing into his victim. The Yak and Leie's Bf 109G-14 went down together.

Four days later, up on the Baltic coast, 13./JG 51 lost its *Staffelkapitän*. One last excerpt from the unit diary;

'11 March: We are expecting our usual Sunday morning fun and games, and aren't disappointed. But this time it's more serious than usual. Russian tanks have broken through and have completely surrounded Danzig-Gotenhafen. We've been on stand-by all week, waiting to transfer to Danzig-Rahmel, but that's now gone by the board. Our advance party has to come back as Ivan is already approaching the field.

'We are ordered to fly fighter-bomber sorties against the advancing enemy tanks. At 0840 hrs the chief takes off with a *Schwarm* to attack tanks reported in the Friedenau-Kölln area. Our chief doesn't return from this mission. He was last seen after completing his attack climbing up into the clouds. He never did like flying in cloud and now they seem to have done for him. But in the evening a Russian radio message is intercepted, according to which Oberleutnant Kalden was brought down by flak and is now in Russian captivity.'

In mid-April 1945, III./JG 51 still had 15 machines at Junkerstroylhof, east of Danzig on the Baltic. Despite the imminent collapse, Oberfeldwebel Helmut Rüffler (right), who commanded 9. *Staffel* for the final fortnight of the war, can still mug it up with Feldwebel Alexander Slomski for a souvenir snapshot

And just 24 hours after Oberleutnant Peter Kalden was shot down, another of JG 51's semi-centurions was lost. Oberfeldwebel Wilhelm Mink was a survivor of the 'happy times' in June-July 1941. After being credited with a couple of RAF machines over the English Channel in the spring of that year, he had opened his Russian score sheet with an SB-2 on the fourth day of *Barbarossa*. Posted to a training unit in 1943, he remained a fighter-instructor for the rest of his career, latterly serving with I./EJG 1.

Wilhem Mink's fabled luck – according to one story, almost certainly apocryphal, he was *twice* shot down off the English coast and *twice* rescued by German U-boats! – finally deserted him on 12 March 1945 when he was caught by RAF fighters while piloting an unarmed Fw 58 'Weihe' on a courier flight over Denmark.

The first of April 1945's four semi-centurion losses was another *Staffelkapitän*. Friedrich Haas had joined II./JG 52 as an unteroffizier in late 1943. On 1 February 1945, the now Leutnant Haas took over the re-formed 4./JG 52 from Hauptmann Erich 'Bubi' Hartmann. Haas' *Staffel* was then redesignated 5./JG 52 on 1 March. As part of II. *Gruppe*, it vacated Veszprem three weeks later, and by the month's end the *Staffel* had retired into Austria.

And it was over the Austrian capital, Vienna, that Leutnant Haas was killed in action against Soviet fighters on 9 April. Forced to bale out of his stricken machine at a height of only 80 metres, there was insufficient time for his parachute to open properly. His final score of 74 earned him a posthumous Knight's Cross before the month was out.

By sheer coincidence, the next two casualties both lost their lives on 24 April, and both while flying jet fighters. But there the similarity ends.

Leutnant Paul-Heinrich Dähne arrived somewhat belatedly on the Russian front with the rest of I./JG 52 early in October 1941, and with a single RAF Blenheim under his belt. Within a fortnight he had added a Soviet DB-3 to the British bomber, and thereafter proceeded to score steadily if not spectacularly. In November 1943 Dähne was appointed *Kapitän* of 2./JG 52, and five months later was awarded the Knight's Cross for his then total of 74.

On 25 May 1944, by which date he had a further seven Red Air Force machines to his credit, Oberleutnant Dähne's 2./JG 52 was selected as one of those *Staffeln* that were to be detached from their parent Russian front *Jagdgruppe* and transferred *en bloc* to Defence of the Reich duties. After a brief period spent re-equipping with Fw 190s, Dähne's *Staffel* was redesignated 12./JG 11. He would lead it until 2 January 1945, when he was selected to replace the fallen Horst-Günther von Fassong (lost in the *Bodenplatte* operation) as *Kommandeur* of III./JG 11.

But then, towards the end of February, Hauptmann Dähne took over II./JG 1, which was about to exchange its late-model Focke-Wulfs for the He 162 lightweight jet fighter. Dähne had little confidence in Heinkel's revolutionary *Volksjäger*, and reportedly delayed his first practice flight in the machine for as long as possible. On 24 April, however, he could put it off no longer. Things very quickly started to go wrong. He got into a sideslip at low altitude, lost control and was killed when he tried to eject.

Unlike Leutnant Dähne, Major Günther Lützow was in at the very beginning of *Barbarossa*, by which time he was already the *Geschwaderkommodore* of JG 3, had 18 western victories to his name (plus five claimed earlier in Spain) and was wearing the Knight's Cross. His score

After their final battles with the Red Air Force over Hungary and Austria, the remaining Bf 109G-10s of II./JG 52 flew west to surrender to US forces at Neubiberg, outside of Munich

sheet lengthened with astonishing rapidity in Russia, earning him both the Oak Leaves and the Swords on the way to his century, which he achieved on 24 October 1941. He was the second pilot (after Werner Mölders) to reach 100, and would add two more Soviet machines to his total before being taken off operational flying.

There followed a succession of staff and training appointments until, in January 1945, he was chosen to speak on behalf of the *Jagdwaffe* at the now-infamous '*Kommodores' Conference*' hosted by Göring in Berlin. The *Reichsmarschall* had, perhaps unwisely, asked his various formation leaders for a summary of their grievances relating to his handling of the Luftwaffe. Oberst Lützow pulled no punches, with the result that Göring stormed from the room shouting his intention to have Lützow court-martialled and shot. It did not come to this, but he was exiled to the backwater of northern Italy to take up the position of *Jafü Oberitalien* ('Fighter-Leader Upper Italy', although by this stage of the war there *were* no Luftwaffe fighters in Italy!).

Lützow was to remain in northern Italy for over two months, before returning to the Reich and joining Adolf Galland's Me 262-equipped JV 44. Despite not having flown operationally for more than two years, and although experiencing some initial problems handling the unfamiliar jet fighter, Oberst Lützow was able to claim at least one kill while flying it. This was a USAAF B-26 downed south of Augsburg on 24 April 1945.

Later that same day he went up again, only to crash at Donauwörth. Although several US fighter pilots put in claims for a Me 262 on this date, the exact circumstances of Lützow's loss are still unresolved. Perhaps he had one more thing in common with Paul-Heinrich Dähne after all – an innate distrust of jet propulsion? For while Galland is on record as claiming that flying the Me 262 was Lützow's 'last great passion', a personal friend contradicted this by maintaining that 'Franzl' Lützow was 'not altogether comfortable' in the cockpit of Messerschmitt's twin-engined jet fighter.

Whatever the truth of the matter, Günther Lützow was undoubtedly an exceptional case. But this account must perforce end with the last of the Russian front semi-centurions to be killed in action. And, perhaps fittingly, his was a career more typical of the many.

Unteroffizier Herbert Bareuther of I./JG 51 had claimed his first kill (a Tupolev SB-2) on the opening morning of *Barbarossa*. Over the course of very nearly the next four years, all spent with the same *Gruppe*, he slowly added 43 more Red Air Force machines to his total – first flying Bf 109Fs, then the Fw 190, before returning to late-model *Gustavs*.

On 2 April 1945 the now Leutnant Bareuther was made *Staffelkapitän* of 14./JG 3. His tenure of office lasted precisely four weeks, during which time he claimed 11 more Soviet machines in operations to the north of Berlin. Then, on 30 April, he failed to return from a low-level attack on a Red Army column advancing northwest along the Baltic coast.

On that very same day the *Führer* committed suicide in his bunker deep under the ruins of Berlin. The name of Adolf Hitler, the architect of Germany's downfall, will be remembered forever. The names of the vast majority of those who fought and died for him on the Russian front – including most of the Luftwaffe's semi-centurions – have already been long forgotten.

Finally, back to the opening minutes of *Barbarossa*. Major Günther Lützow's first 'Russian front victory (an 'I-18') was claimed just after dawn on the morning of 22 June 1941. His 84th, and last (a MiG-1), just after midday on 21 May 1942. Widely respected as a true professional, Oberst Lützow was to lose his life flying a Me 262 jet fighter of JV 44 just two weeks before the war's end

APPENDICES

	Eastern Front Victories (1)	Others (2)	German Cross in Gold (3)	Knight's Cross (4)	Eastern Front JG(s) (5)	Lost (6)	
Lt Leopold Steinbatz	99	-	22/01/42	14/02/42/42 (7)	52	15/06/42	MiA/E
Maj Heinz Bär*	96	124	08/06/42	02/07/41/27 (8)	51/77	-	
Hptm Heinrich Höfemeier*	96	-	19/03/42	05/04/42/41	51	07/08/43	KiA/E
Lt Hermann Schleinhege*	96	-	20/03/44	19/02/45/c90	3/54	-	
Maj Reinhard Seiler*	96	4	15/10/41	20/12/41/42 (9)	54	-	
Hptm Wolfgang Tonne	96	26	21/08/42	06/09/42/73 (10)	53	20/04/43	KAS/M
Lt Anton Döbele*	94	-	31/08/43	26/03/44(†)	54	11/11/43	KiA/E
Maj/ Diethelm von Eichel-Streiber*	94	-	17/10/43	05/04/44/71	77/51	-	
Obfw Rudolf Müller	94	-	27/05/42	19/06/42/46	5	19/04/43	PoW/A
Maj Rudolf Resch*	94	-	27/07/42	06/09/42/50	52/51	11/07/43	KiA/E
Oblt Max-Hellmuth Ostermann	93	9	-	04/09/41/29 (11)	54	09/08/42	KiA/E
Oblt Hans Schleef	92	6	04/05/42	09/05/42/41	3/5	31/12/44	KiA/W
Oblt Anton Resch	91	-	01/01/45	07/04/45/?	52	-	
Oblt Horst Hannig	90	8	24/11/41	09/05/42/48 (12)	54	15/05/43	KiA/W
Lt Rudolf Rademacher*	90	36	25/03/43	30/09/44/95	54	-	
Maj Wolfgang Späte*	90	9	09/12/41	05/10/41/45 (13)	54	-	
Maj Kurt Ubben	90	20	09/12/41	04/09/41/28 (14)	77	27/04/44	KiA/W
Hptm Robert Weiss*	c90	c31	12/07/43	26/03/44/70 (15)	54	29/12/44	KiA/W
Obstlt Friedrich-Karl Müller	87	53	15/11/43	14/09/41/c30 (16)	53/3	29/05/44	KAS/R
Lt Edmund Rossmann	87	6	22/01/42	19/03/42/42	52	09/07/43	PoW/E
Oblt Georg Schentke	86	4	24/09/42	04/09/41/30	3	25/12/42	MiA/E
Lt Friedrich Wachowiak	86	-	22/01/42	05/04/42/46	52	16/07/44	KiA/W
Lt Ulrich Wöhnert*	86	-	14/11/43	06/12/44/86	54	-	
Hptm Paul-Heinrich Dähne*	85	14	17/10/43	06/04/44/74	52/11	24/04/45	KAS/R
Lt Gerhard Köppen	85	-	15/12/41	18/12/41/40 (17)	52	05/05/42	MiA/E
Maj Hartmann Grasser	85	18	19/09/42	04/09/41/29 (18)	51	-	
Hptm Eberhard von Boremski	84	6	12/07/43	03/05/42/43	3	-	
Lt Heinz Ewald	84	1	?	20/04/45/82	52	-	
Oberst Günther Lützow	84	19	?	18/09/40/15 (19)	3	24/04/45	KiA/R
Fhj-Obfw Werner Quast	84	-	23/07/43	31/12/43/?	52	07/08/43	PoW/E
Oblt Oskar Romm	82	10	17/10/43	29/02/44/76	52	-	
Lt Walter Zellot	82	3	15/10/42(†)	03/09/42/84	53	10/09/42	KiA/E
Lt Hugo Broch*	81	-	17/10/43	12/03/45/79	54	-	
Lt Josef Jennewein*	81	5	12/04/43	05/12/43(†)	51	26/07/43	MiA/E
Oblt Hermann Lücke*	81	-	16/08/43	06/04/44(†)	51	08/11/43	DoW/E
Lt Willi Nemitz	81	-	27/10/42	11/03/43/54	52	11/04/43	KiA/E
Lt Rudolf Wagner*	81	-	17/10/43	26/03/44(†)	51	11/12/43	MiA/E
Lt Walter Ohlrogge	80	3	03/11/42	04/11/41/39	3	-	
Lt Herbert Bachnick	79	1	05/02/44	27/07/44/79	52	07/08/44	KiA/E
Hptm Hans Götz*	79	3	02/07/42	23/12/42/48	54	04/08/43	KiA/E
Lt Otto Würfel*	79	-	26/12/43	04/05/44/79	51	23/02/44	PoW/E
Oblt Heinrich Klöpper	78	16	21/08/42	04/09/42/65	51	29/11/43	MiA/R

Name							
Oblt Gerhard Loos	c78	c14	17/10/43	05/02/44/85	54	06/03/44	KiA/R
Obstlt Helmut Bennemann	77	15	27/07/42	02/10/42/50	52	-	
Maj Franz Beyer	77	6	19/09/42	30/08/41/32	3	11/02/44	KiA/R
Oberst Walter Dahl	77	51	02/12/42	11/03/44/64 (20)	3	-	
Lt Johann-Hermann Meier	76	1	27/10/43	06/01/45(†)	51/52	15/03/44	KAS/W
Obfw Helmut Rüffler	76	12	03/12/42	23/12/42/50	3/51	-	
Hptm Edwin Thiel*	76	-	09/09/42	16/04/43/51	51/52	14/07/44	KiA/E
Lt Johann Bunzek	75	-	14/11/43	06/04/44(†)	52	11/12/43	KiA/E
Hptm Friedrich Geisshardt	75	27	24/04/42	30/08/41/26 (21)	LG 2/77	06/04/43	DoW/W
Lt Helmut Grollmus*	75	-	12/12/43	06/10/44(†)	54	19/06/44	KiA/E
Lt Hans-Joachim Kroschinski*	75	1	27/10/43	17/04/45/76	54	-	
Obstlt Erich Leie*	75	46	20/10/42	01/08/41/21	51/77	07/03/45	KiA/E
Lt Leopold Münster	75	20	03/10/42	21/12/42/52 (22)	3	08/05/44	KiA/R
Lt Otto Gaiser*	74	-	28/01/44	09/06/44(†)	51	22/01/44	MiA/E
Lt Friedrich Haas	74	-	26/07/44	?/04/45(†)	52	09/04/45	KiA/E
Hptm Heinrich Krafft*	74	4	19/01/42	18/03/42/46	51	14/12/42	KiA/E
Fw Karl-Heinz Meltzer	74	-	17/10/43(†)	-	52	14/08/43	MiA/E
Hptm Joachim Wandel	73	2	27/07/42	21/08/42/64	54	07/10/42	KiA/E
Oblt Anton Lindner*	72	1	27/05/42	08/04/44/62	51	-	
Hptm Maximilian Mayerl*	72	4	27/11/42	14/12/43/66	51	-	
Maj Wolfgang Ewald	71	2	03/10/42	09/12/42/50	52/3	14/07/43	PoW/E
Hptm Horst-Günther von Fassong*	71	4	17/10/43	27/07/44/c100	51/11	01/01/45	KiA/W
Lt Hans Fuss	71	-	10/07/42	23/08/42/60	3	10/11/42	DoW/E
Oblt Heinz Kemethmüller	70	19	03/10/42	02/10/42/59	3/26	-	
Oblt Peter Kalden*	69	-	01/01/45	06/12/44/64	51	11/03/45	PoW/E
Maj Heinz Lange*	69	1	17/05/43	18/11/44/70	54/51	-	
Oberst Karl-Gottfried Nordmann*	69	9	?	01/08/41/31 (23)	51	-	
Oblt Ernst Weismann	69	-	?	21/08/42(†)	51	13/08/42	MiA/E
Oblt Kurt Dombacher*	68	-	01/10/44	08/04/45/?	5/51	-	
Hptm Heinrich Jung*	68	-	17/11/42	12/11/43(†)	54	30/07/43	KiA/E
Obfw Kurt Ratzlaff	68	-	11/05/42	-	52	29/09/42	PoW/E
Lt Hans Strelow	68	-	?	18/03/42/52 (24)	51	22/05/42	KiA/E
Hptm Herbert Findeisen*	67	-	26/11/43	29/02/44/36	54	-	
Obfw Karl Fuchs*	67	-	24/10/42	-	54	10/10/43	MiA/E
Obfw Karl Hammerl	67	-	21/08/42	19/09/42/50	52	02/03/43	MiA/E
Oberst Herbert Ihlefeld	67	56	?	13/09/40/21 (25)	LG 2/77/52	-	
Obfw Hubert Strassl*	67	-	16/08/43	12/11/43(†)	51	08/07/43	KiA/E
Lt Rudi Linz*	c67	c3	01/01/45	?/03/45(†)	5	09/02/45	KiA/W
Oblt Gustav Denk	66	1	23/12/42	14/03/43(†)	52	13/02/43	KiA/E
Hptm Gustav Frielinghaus	66	8	24/09/42	05/02/44/c70	3	-	
Hptm Alfred Teumer*	66	10	17/10/43	19/08/44/76	54	04/10/44	KAS/R
Oblt Ernst Süss	c66	c2	02/07/42	04/09/42/50	52	20/12/43	KiA/R
Lt Hans Döbrich	65	5	15/10/42	19/09/43/65	5	-	
Oblt Heinrich Füllgrabe	65	-	11/05/42	02/10/42/52	52	30/01/45	KiA/E
Lt Waldemar Semelka	65	-	21/08/42	04/09/42 (†)	52	21/08/42	MiA/E
Oblt Otto Tange*	65	3	24/11/41	19/03/42/41	51	30/07/43	KiA/E
Obstlt Hubertus von Bonin*	64	9	27/10/42	21/12/42/51	54/52	15/12/43	KiA/E
Obfw Berthold Grassmuck	64	1	13/08/42	19/09/42/56	52	28/10/42	KiA/E
Obfw Wilhelm Mink	64	8	04/02/42	19/03/42/40	51	12/03/45	KAS/W
Lt Viktor Petermann	64	-	23/07/43	29/02/44/60	52	-	
Maj Karl-Heinz Schnell*	63	9	10/10/42	01/08/41/29	51	-	

Name						
Obfw Heinrich Hoffmann	62	1	-	12/08/41/40 (26)	51	03/10/41 MiA/E
Obstlt Anton Mader*	62	24	02/01/42	23/07/42/40	77/54	-
Lt Helmut Neumann*	62	-	01/01/45	12/03/45/62	5	-
Oblt Otto Wessling	62	21	?	03/09/42/50 (27)	3	19/04/44 KiA/R
Oblt Hans Grünberg	61	21	31/08/43	08/07/44/70	3	-
Obfw Gerhard Beutin*	60	-	25/03/43(†) -		54	01/02/43 ?/?
Hptm Josef Haiböck	60	17	17/10/43	09/06/44/77	52	-
Lt Reinhold Hoffmann*	60	6	14/11/43	28/01/45(†)	54	24/05/44 KiA/R
Maj Bernd Gallowitsch	59	5	?	24/01/42/42	51	-
Obfw Alexander Preinfalk	59	19	03/10/42	14/10/42/50	77	12/12/44 KiA/R
Lt Herbert Friebel*	58	-	08/09/42	24/01/43/51	51	15/05/44 KiA/E
Lt Helmut Haberda	58	-	02/08/43(†) -		52	08/05/43 KiA/E
Lt Walter Jahnke	58	-	28/01/44	-	52	-
Lt Adolf Nehrig	58	-	01/01/45	-	52	-
Obfw Karl Steffen	58	1	11/05/42	01/07/42/44	52	08/08/43 MiA/E
Obfw Heinz-Wilhelm Ahnert	57	-	27/07/42	23/08/42(†)	52	23/08/42 KiA/E
Lt Herbert Broennle	57	1	15/06/42	14/03/43/57	54	04/07/43 KiA/M
Obfw Heinrich Dittlmann*	57	-	17/10/43	-	51	23/02/44 KiA/E
Lt Erwin Fleig	57	9	-	12/08/41/26	51	29/05/42 PoW/E
Lt Horst Forbrig*	57	1	31/08/43	-	54	12/06/44 MiA/W
Maj Siegfried Freytag	57	45	25/01/43	03/07/42/49	77	-
Oblt Alfred Heckmann	57	14	09/04/42	19/09/42/50	3/26	-
Lt Karl Munz	57	3	12/12/43	?	52	-
Maj Fritz Losigkeit*	c57	c11	17/10/43	?/04/45/68	51/77	-
Lt Manfred Eberwein	56	-	01/01/45	-	52/54	-
Lt Hans Ellendt	56	-	05/02/44	-	52	-
Hptm Günther Fink	56	-	27/10/42	14/03/43/46	54	15/05/43 MiA/R
Maj Walter Hoeckner	56	12	02/07/42	06/04/44/65	77	25/08/44 KAS/R
Fw Helmut Holtz*	56	-	28/01/44	-	51	18/04/44 MiA/E
Obfw Helmut Schönfelder*	56	-	01/01/45	31/03/45/?	51	-
Fw Karl-Friedrich Schumacher	56	-	08/02/43	-	52	31/05/44 KiA/E
Lt Herbert Bareuther*	55	-	05/02/44	?/04/45/?	51/3	30/04/45 KiA/E
Hptm Franz Eckerle	55	4	-	18/09/41/30 (28)	54	14/02/42 MiA/E
Obfw Alfred Franke	55	4	25/09/42	29/10/42(†)	53	09/09/42 KiA/E
Obfw Wilhelm Freuwörth	55	3	17/11/42	05/01/43/56	52	-
Maj Wilhelm Leppla	55	13	09/12/41	27/07/41/27	51/6	-
Obfw Wilhelm Philipp*	55	26	27/10/42	26/03/44/61	54	-
Lt Franz Schwaiger	55	12	29/10/42	29/10/42/52	3	24/04/44 KiA/R
Uffz Gabriel Tautscher*	55	-	17/10/43	-	51	12/01/44 KiA/E
Obfw Edmund Wagner	55	-	-	17/11/41(†)	51	13/11/41 KiA/E
Oblt Siegfried Engfer	c55	c3	?	02/10/42/52	3	-
Lt Wilhelm Theimann*	c55	-	31/03/43	-	51	29/07/43 KiA/E
Fw Wilhelm Hauswirth	54	-	23/07/43(†) -		52	05/07/43 MiA/E
Lt Heinz Leber*	54	-	17/06/42	29/02/44(†)	51	01/06/43 KiA/E
Obfw Kurt Olsen*	54	-	31/08/43	-	54	-
Hptm Emil Omert	54	16	17/02/43	19/03/42/40	77	24/04/44 KiA/E
Lt Alfred Rauch*	54	6	23/07/43	09/04/45/53	51	-
Oblt Eugen-Ludwig Zweigart	c54	c15	17/11/42	22/01/43/54	54	08/06/44 KiA/W
Obfw Albert Brunner	53	-	04/06/43(†) 03/07/43(†)		5	07/05/43 KiA/A
Hptm Lutz-Wilhelm Burckhardt	53	5	?	22/09/42/53	77	-
Lt Hans-Joachim Heyer	53	-	04/08/42	25/11/42(†)	54	09/11/42 MiA/E

Hptm Karl Sattig	53	-	05/06/42	19/09/42(†)	54	10/08/42	MiA/E
Maj Horst Carganico	52	8	18/05/42	25/09/41/27	5	27/05/44	KiA/W
Oblt Kurt Ebener	52	5	18/03/43	07/04/43/52	3	23/08/44	PoW/W
Lt Ludwig Häfner	52	-	25/09/42	21/12/42(†)	3	10/11/42	MiA/E
Lt Johann Badum	51	3	03/10/42	15/10/42/51	77	11/01/43	KiA/M
Obfw Kurt Knappe	51	5	24/09/42	03/11/42/51	51	03/09/43	KiA/W
Hptm Hans Roehrig	51	24	?	02/10/42/51	53	07/07/43	MiA/M
Lt Hermann Wolf	51	6	23/07/43	?	52	-	
Lt Friedrich Rupp	50	3	27/10/42	24/01/43/50	54	15/05/43	KiA/R
Hptm Adalbert Sommer	50	3	03/10/42	-	52/?	14/03/44	KiA/E

KEY

(1) – includes US aircraft claimed over Rumania & Hungary

(2) – kills claimed in West, Mediterranean, Balkans & Reich

(3) – date of award

(4) – date of award/number of victories at time of award

(5) – units during pilot's Russian front service only

(6) – date of loss, plus detail/theatre, i.e.

KiA – Killed in action	E – East
MiA – Missing in action	W – West
KAS – Killed on active service	A – Arctic
DoW – Died of wounds	R – Reich
PoW – Prisoner of war	M – Mediterranean

(*) – after pilot's name indicates his score includes kills on Fw 190

(†) – after date of award indicates conferred posthumously

(c) – circa

(7) also Oak Leaves (2/6/42/83) & Swords (23/6/42(†))

(8) also Oak Leaves (14/8/41/60) & Swords (16/2/42/90)

(9) also Oak Leaves (2/3/44/100)

(10) also Oak Leaves (24/9/42/101)

(11) also Oak Leaves (10/3/42/62) & Swords (17/5/42/100)

(12) also Oak Leaves (3/1/44(†))

(13) also Oak Leaves (23/04/42/72)

(14) also Oak Leaves (12/3/42/69)

(15) also Oak Leaves (12/3/45(†))

(16) also Oak Leaves (23/9/42/100)

(17) also Oak Leaves (27/2/42/72)

(18) also Oak Leaves (31/8/43/103)

(19) also Oak Leaves (20/7/41/42) & Swords (11/10/41/92)

(20) also Oak Leaves (1/2/45/100)

(21) also Oak Leaves (23/6/42/79)

(22) also Oak Leaves (12/5/44(†))

(23) also Oak Leaves (16/9/41/59)

(24) also Oak Leaves (24/3/42/66)

(25) also Oak Leaves (27/6/41/40) & Swords (24/4/42/101)

(26) also Oak Leaves (19/10/41(†))

(27) also Oak Leaves (20/07/44(†))

(28) also Oak Leaves (12/03/42(†))

COLOUR PLATES

1

Bf 109G-4 'White 3' of Leutnant Leopold Münster, 4./JG 3, Varvarovka/Ukraine, Summer 1943

During its second tour of the Russian front, from spring 1942 to late summer 1943, II./JG 3 gradually converted from Bf 109Fs onto early model *Gustavs*. 'Poldi' Münster's 'White 3' is typical of the *Gruppe's* machines towards the end of this period. It bears no unit markings, and the white of the numeral and fuselage *Balkenkreuz* has been toned down – an indication of the ever-growing danger posed by Soviet ground-attack aircraft post-Stalingrad. II./JG 3 would be transferred to Defence of the Reich in August 1943, where Leutnant Münster achieved further successes before being killed in a mid-air collision with a B-24 on 8 May 1944.

2

Bf 109F-4 'Black 6' of Oberfeldwebel Alfred Heckmann, 5./JG 3, Mariyevka/Voronezh Province, July 1942

Depicted a year prior to Münster's machine immediately above, this *Friedrich* illustrates the difference that a mere 12 months can make. In mid-1942, II./JG 3 was still advancing towards the Don. Its fighters wore full unit markings – the Udet *Geschwader's* 'Winged U' on the engine cowling and II. *Gruppe's* black and white gyronny device below the windshield. Note also the pilot's current score recorded on the rudder – 38 white bars, the last four of which represent a quartet of Bostons despatched in as many minutes on the morning of 10 July. 'Fred' Heckmann himself would survive the war, serving as a *Staffelkapitän* with JG 26 in the west during 1944-45, and latterly flying the Fw 190D-9 'Long nose'.

3

Bf 109G-4 'Black Chevron and Bar' of Major Wolfgang Ewald, *Gruppenkommandeur* III./JG 3, Gorlovka/Ukraine, January 1943

This G-4 'gunboat' was one of several machines flown by Wolfgang Ewald during his *Gruppe's* support of the Stalingrad airlift operations in the winter of 1942-43. It would be severely damaged in a crash-landing at Kharkov in April 1943 (not piloted by Ewald), and while undergoing repair, would be converted into a G-12 two-seat trainer. Like 'Fred' Heckmann, Wolfgang 'Pecenio' Ewald would survive the war, albeit in very different circumstances. Downed by Soviet flak northeast of Byelgorod on 14 July 1943, he parachuted into Russian captivity, where he would remain until long after hostilities had ceased.

4

**Bf 109F-2 'Black 5' of Oberleutnant Franz Beyer,
Staffelkapitän 8./JG 3, Byelaya-Zerkov/Ukraine, July 1941**

Although yet to receive its Russian front yellow theatre markings, Beyer's *Friedrich* already displays III./JG 3's 'Battleaxe' shield on the engine nacelle and its pilot's personal score on the rudder. The latter is deceptive, however, for Beyer has included machines destroyed on the ground among his total. Apart from the first three bars for aerial kills claimed prior to *Barbarossa*, it is difficult to distinguish from the original print just which is which. But the number of aircraft shot down appears to be 30+, which would establish the date as circa late July 1941. In May 1943 Major Beyer was appointed *Kommandeur* of the newly activated IV./JG 3. He achieved just three more western victories to add to his Russian front tally of 77 before being killed in action by RAF Spitfires over Holland on 11 February 1944.

5

**Bf 109F-4 'Yellow 4' of Oberfeldwebel Eberhard von
Boremski, 9./JG 3, Zhuguyev/Ukraine, May 1942**

When III./JG 3 returned to the Russian front in May 1942 after re-equipment in the Reich, many pilots were flying F-4s originally destined for the Mediterranean theatre. Hence the unusual camouflage scheme shown here, which consisted of desert tan upper surfaces and light blue undersides (the standard North African finish), with large segments of dark green and light grey applied to the former to make the machines more suited to the Russian terrain. Oberleutnant von Boremski was severely injured in an emergency landing on 30 May 1943 while serving as *Staffelkapitän* of 7./JG 3, and spent the remainder of the war primarily in training roles.

6

**Bf 109F-4 'Yellow 3' of Feldwebel Rudolf Müller, 6./JG 5,
Petsamo/Arctic Front, June 1942**

A splinter camouflage finish of a different kind was worn at one stage by the *Friedrichs* of II./JG 5 in the far north. Described by one source as a 'combination of stone grey and dark moss green', this was presumably intended to blend in with the rocky Arctic tundra landscape of the summer months. 6./JG 5 was the undisputed *Experten-Staffel* of the far north, and 'Rudi' Müller was its first big ace. Although 'Yellow 3' is not wearing II./JG 5's four-leaf clover badge (usually carried on the nacelle immediately aft of the spinner), nor a II. *Gruppe* horizontal bar aft of the fuselage cross, it does sport Müller's personal emblem below the windscreen.

7

**Bf 109G-2/R6 'Yellow 10' of Feldwebel Hans Döbrich,
6./JG 5, Salmijärvi/Arctic Front, Spring 1943**

II./JG 5 was equipped with *Gustavs* in early 1943, and each machine was quickly given an individual coat of winter camouflage (ranging from dapple, 'scribble' or splinter to solid white). This 'gunboat', flown by Feldwebel Hans Döbrich, another of 6. *Staffel's* leading NCO *Experten*, is a typical example. Although it was no longer customary to display a pilot's score on the rudder of his aircraft (Döbrich claimed his 50th on 23 March 1943), 'Yellow 10' does wear the clover emblem of II./JG 5, which is again featured in 6. *Staffel's* badge – 'Mickey Mouse the *Rata* breaker' – below the cockpit. Hans Döbrich was taken off operations after being severely wounded over Petsamo Fjord on 16 July 1943.

8

**Bf 109G-2/R6 'Yellow 3' of Oberfeldwebel Rudolf Müller,
6./JG 5, Salmijärvi/Arctic Front, April 1943**

Finished in a very similar temporary winter scheme to Döberich's 'Yellow 10', 'Rudi' Müller's 'gunboat' is as devoid of unit markings as his earlier F-4 (see profile 6) – even his personal cat motif and rudder tally have now gone by the board. It was in this anonymous-looking 'Yellow 3' (Werk-Nr. 14810) that Müller was forced to make an emergency landing behind enemy lines on the frozen 'Great Lake' east of Murmansk on 19 April 1943. At the time of his loss (he was never to return from Soviet captivity), Müller's total of 94 made him JG 5's highest scoring ace, and had already earned him a nomination for the Oak Leaves.

9

**Bf 109G-6 'Black Double Chevron' of Major Erich Leie,
Gruppenkommandeur I./JG 51, Orsha/Central Sector,
Winter 1943-44**

Other than being the mount of a *Gruppenkommandeur* (double chevron) on the Russian front (yellow theatre markings), this winter-camouflaged *Gustav* offers few clues as to its pilot's identity. It is, in fact, the machine flown by Major Erich Leie, who had already made his name on the Channel front with JG 2 'Richthofen', prior to assuming command of I./JG 51 in January 1943. Leie would remain at the head of I./JG 51 for almost two years – during which time he claimed 71 victories – before being appointed *Geschwaderkommodore* of JG 77 in December 1944. He was killed in action over Silesia on 7 March 1945. Like 'Rudi' Müller, he too had been nominated for the Oak Leaves.

10

**Bf 109F-2 'Black 11' of Feldwebel Anton Lindner, 2./JG 51,
Stara Bychov/Central Sector, July 1941**

Another fighter-bomber, albeit this time armed with four 50-kg bombs and depicted during the opening months of *Barbarossa*, this F-2 is finished in the soft green dapple typical of the *Friedrichs* of the period. Note too the *Geschwader* emblem introduced by *Kommodore* Werner Mölders shortly before the campaign began. With but one short interlude as *Staffelkapitän* of 4./EJG 1 (November 1944 – January 1945), 'Toni' Lindner served with JG 51 throughout almost the entire war. And although an acknowledged *Jabo* specialist, he also racked up 73 aerial kills – all but one against the Russians.

11

**Bf 109F-2 'Yellow 7' of Oberleutnant Heinrich Krafft,
Staffelkapitän 3./JG 51, Stolzy/Central Sector, March
1942**

Back to winter white for this *Friedrich* (and note too the removal of the main wheel leg doors to prevent the build-up of impacted snow when taxiing). The 46 victories carefully recorded on the rudder – all but the first four scored in the east – earned 'Gaudi' Krafft the Knight's Cross on 18 March 1942. On 1 June he was appointed *Kommandeur* of I./JG 51, which he led for more than six months. His final overall score was standing at 78 when he was brought down by Soviet flak southwest of Rzhev on 14 December 1942 while flying one of his *Gruppe's* new Fw 190A-3s.

12

Bf 109F-2 'Black 3' of Oberleutnant Hartmann Grasser, *Staffelkapitän* 5./JG 51, Shatalovka-West/Central Sector, August 1941

Generally similar in overall finish to Lindner's machine (profile 10), Grasser's 'Black 3' displays several differences in detail. The most obvious is perhaps the placement of the II. *Gruppe* horizontal bar *ahead* of the fuselage cross in order to accommodate the *Gruppe's* 'Weeping Raven' crest on the rear fuselage. Note also Grasser's scoreboard on the rudder – 26 victories, the first seven of which were claimed in the west prior to *Barbarossa*. No 29 (an R-3 reconnaissance biplane downed on 2 September) would earn him the Knight's Cross, and his 103rd and last (a Spitfire over Tunisia in March 1943) would result in the Oak Leaves. Grasser subsequently served in various operational and staff posts until the end of the war.

13

Bf 109F-2 'Black 10' of Leutnant Hans Strelow, *Staffelkapitän* 5./JG 51, Szolzy/Central Sector, February 1942

A lot can happen in six months! The 27-year-old Hartmann Grasser, veteran of the Battles of France and Britain, has been appointed *Kommandeur* of II. *Gruppe*, and 5./JG 51 is now in the hands of nineteen-year-old Hans Strelow. Also, high summer has given way to the depths of winter, and the *Staffel's Friedrichs* are garbed in overall white (effectively obscuring that tell-tale *Gruppe* bar). Two things remain the same, however – the *Geschwader* badge on the cowling and the pilot's score on the rudder. In Strelow's case, this shows that he has racked up the hitherto obligatory 40 and is now enquiring when his Knight's Cross will arrive (see photograph on page 24). The answer is 18 March (for his then 52 kills), followed six days later by the Oak Leaves (for 66). Hans Strelow would wear the latter for just two months before being reported missing on 22 May 1942.

14

Bf 109F-2 'Black 3' of Oberfeldwebel Otto Tange, 5./JG 51, Bryansk/Central Sector, May 1942

Just six days prior to Strelow's loss, one of the pilots of his *Staffel* had reached his half-century. It was during a Stuka escort mission on 16 May 1942 that Otto Tange claimed a Red Air Force Boston and two of the bomber formation's escorting fighters to take his overall total to 51, as recorded here on the rudder of his 'Black 3'. The same scoreboard also reveals that Tange's first three victories were gained in the west (RAF fighters over the Channel and North Sea). In 1943, the now Leutnant Otto Tange was transferred to JG 51's Fw 190-equipped *Stabsstaffel*. He was killed on 30 July of that year when his machine took a direct flak hit. Tange's final Russian front score was 65.

15

Bf 109F-2 'Black 4' of Feldwebel Kurt Knappe, 5./JG 51, Orel/Central Sector, August 1942

Yet another of 5./JG 51's semi-centurion NCOs, Gefreiter Kurt Knappe had claimed his first victory – an Ilyushin DB-3

bomber – on 26 July 1941. He topped the half-century some 15 months later on 4 October 1942. Although his *Friedrich* is generally similar to Tange's, it does display one slight variation – that rogue II. *Gruppe* horizontal bar has edged even further forward, and is now displayed ahead of both the fuselage cross *and* the machine's individual number. In November 1942 Kurt Tange was posted to JG 2 'Richthofen' on the Channel coast. There, he would achieve just five more victories (including three US heavy bombers) before being killed in action against Spitfires on 3 September 1943.

16

Bf 109F-2 'Black Chevron and Circle' of Hauptmann Richard Leppla, *Gruppenkommandeur* III./JG 51, Yuchnov/Central Sector, August 1942

It was in this machine, wearing a decidedly darker finish than the *Friedrichs* illustrated hitherto – and carrying fuselage markings that suggest it had been 'borrowed' from the *Gruppen*-TO (Technical, or Engineering, Officer) – that Hauptmann Richard Leppla was seriously injured when he collided with a Ju 52/3m during take-off from Yuchnov on 7 August 1942. Leppla had embarked upon *Barbarossa* with 13 victories already to his credit, and had added 55 Soviet aircraft to his tally by the time of his accident. There were to be no more. Upon recovery, Leppla served in various staff and training positions before being made *Geschwaderkommodore* of JG 6 for the final two weeks of the war.

17

Bf 109F-2 'Yellow 1' of Oberfeldwebel Edmund Wagner, 9./JG 51, Yuchnov/Central Sector, October 1941

Another machine possibly on loan from its rightful owner. Early Luftwaffe regulations stipulated that a *Staffelkapitän* was always allocated the aircraft bearing the numeral '1', but as the war progressed, this 'rule' became increasingly redundant. Whatever the truth of the matter, it was in this 'Yellow 1', devoid of all unit badges, that Edmund Wagner – one of the first Russian front semi-centurions (his 50th went down on 28 October) – was himself killed in action against Soviet Pe-2 bombers on 13 November 1941. Only the second semi-centurion to be lost, Wagner's final total of 55 earned him a posthumous Knight's Cross.

18

Bf 109F-2 'Black Double Chevron' of Oberleutnant Karl-Gottfried Nordmann, *Gruppenkommandeur* IV./JG 51, Shatalovka/Central Sector, August 1941

Although this somewhat darkly oversprayed F-2 does not feature a rudder scoreboard (Nordmann was, in fact, only seven short of becoming an Russian front semi-centurion by month's end), it does display a wealth of other markings – the *Geschwader* badge on the cowling, *Gruppe* shield below the cockpit, *Kommandeur's* chevrons and *Gruppe* symbol (a second, smaller, cross behind the *Balkenkreuz*). Like Krafft (profile 11), Nordmann's operational career also came to an end shortly after he converted onto the Fw 190 – although not in the same way. Holding himself responsible for a mid-air collision that killed his wingman on 17 January 1943, Nordmann never flew on ops again. He spent the closing months of the war in various staff appointments, latterly as 'Inspectorate Day Fighters East'.

19

Bf 109F-2 'Black 3' of Feldwebel Heinz Klöpper, 11./JG 51, Minsk/Central Sector, July 1941

Heinz Klöpper's rather worn looking 'Black 3' has exactly five bars adorning its rudder – the first, a Spitfire downed off Dungeness on 5 October 1940, and the fifth, claimed on 30 June 1941, identified as an 'R-10 recce aircraft' (although more probably a Sukhoi Su-2 light bomber). In all, Klöpper would achieve 78 Russian front kills before being transferred to the west, firstly to JG 2 'Richthofen' in France and then as *Staffelkapitän* to the new 7./JG 1 in Defence of the Reich. Oberleutnant Heinz Klöpper was reported missing after a dogfight with Lightnings over Holland on 29 November 1943.

20

Bf 109G-2/R6 'Black Double Chevron' of Hauptmann Helmut Bennemann, *Gruppenkommandeur* I./JG 52, Maikop/Caucasus, October 1942

This densely dappled 'gunboat' not only wears JG 52's 'Winged sword' crest, but also retains I. *Gruppe's* by now decidedly anachronistic 'Black hand clutching a Spitfire over the North Sea' emblem (as *Gruppen-Adjutant* for much of 1940-41, Bennemann had scored his first 11 victories during this period). He had reached his half-century by early October 1942, and would take his Russian front total to 77 before being appointed *Geschwaderkommodore* of JG 53 in November 1943. Remaining in this post until war's end, he added just four more Western machines to his tally, giving him a final overall score of 92.

21

Bf 109G-6 'Black 4' of Oberleutnant Paul-Heinrich Dähne, *Staffelkapitän* 2./JG 52, Zilistea/Rumania, May 1944

Paul-Heinrich 'Sarotti' Dähne joined 2./JG 52 in Russia in 1942, becoming *Staffelkapitän* on 13 November 1943. Then, in May 1944, 2./JG 52 was selected as one of the *Staffeln* to be withdrawn *en bloc* from the Russian front for incorporation into the Defence of the Reich organisation. After converting onto the Fw 190, Dähne's unit was redesignated 12./JG 11 and promptly despatched back to the Russian front! There, he claimed five more victories to add to the 80 he had already achieved with JG 51. Returning to the west in September 1944, 'Sarotti' Dähne served as *Gruppenkommandeur* of both III./JG 11 and II./JG 1 before being killed flying an He 162 'Volksjäger' on 24 April 1945.

22

Bf 109F-2 'Yellow 1' of Oberleutnant Rudolf Resch, *Staffelkapitän* 6./JG 52, Kamary/Central Sector, July 1941

Back to the opening weeks of *Barbarossa* for 'Rudi' Resch's 'Yellow 1' – a *Friedrich* in standard pale dapple finish. It carries the *Geschwader* badge beneath the windscreen, and II./JG 52's trademark broad yellow theatre band, covering the entire aft fuselage from *Balkenkreuz* to tailfin root. Note also the four kill bars on the rudder. These represent the four Tupolev bombers claimed by Resch in the first five weeks of the war in the east. Although a (relatively) slow starter, the later Major Rudolf Resch more than made up for it, claiming 73 victories with JG 52, and then adding a further 21 as *Kommandeur* of IV./JG 51 – taking him to just six short of his century by the time of his death in action during *Zitadelle*.

23

Bf 109F-4 'White 9' of Unteroffizier Eduard Rossmann, 7./JG 52, Mironovka/Ukraine, September 1941

Presenting an altogether different appearance from the previous *Friedrich*, Rossmann's 'White 9' wears a much darker dapple, has a yellow cowling and sports III. *Gruppe's* new unit badge and distinctly oversized wavy bar aft fuselage marking. The rudder bears witness to the pilot's 14 Russian front victories to date (the last three all claimed on 7 September). After scoring 87 kills in the east, 'Paule' Rossmann's operational career also came to an end during *Zitadelle* on 9 July 1943, when he deliberately landed behind enemy lines to try to rescue a downed fellow pilot but was unable to take off again and was himself captured.

24

Bf 109G-10 'White 3' of Leutnant Heinz Ewald, *Staffelkapitän* 7./JG 52, Veszprem/Hungary, February 1945

The identity of the pilot of this otherwise anonymous late model Bf 109G is revealed by the personal emblem beneath the cockpit – an 'E' followed by a sow is a phonetic pun for 'Esau', the nickname of Heinz Ewald. This marking was carried in one form or another on most, if not all, of Ewald's machines (see photo on page 64 for an earlier example). One of the best of the younger generation pilots, Ewald reached his half-century on 29 December 1944 and was appointed *Kapitän* of 7./JG 52 on 15 February 1945. He survived the war with a final total of 84 Russian front victories.

25

Bf 109G-2 'Black 12' of Leutnant Walter Zellot, *Staffelkapitän* 2./JG 53, Tusow/Stalingrad Front, August 1942

Although most of JG 53's various stints on the Russian front were of fairly limited duration, the *Geschwader* nonetheless managed to produce a handful of semi-centurions. Among them was Walter Zellot, whose *Gustav* is shown here during I. *Gruppe's* second tour in the east when they supported 6. *Armee's* advance on Stalingrad. At this time Zellot was I./JG 53's highest scorer, receiving the Knight's Cross for his 84 victories (all but three claimed against the Red Air Force) on 3 September. He would add just one more kill to his tally before he himself was brought down by Soviet flak during a low-level attack near Stalingrad exactly a week later. At the time of his loss Zellot was not flying 'Black 12' but the oddly marked '10' machine, on which the '1' was in black and the '0' apparently in white!

26

Bf 109F-2 'Black Double Chevron' of Hauptmann Franz Eckerle, *Gruppenkommandeur* I./JG 54, Krasnogvardeisk/Leningrad Front, January 1942

From summer on the southern sector to winter on the northern front – Franz Eckerle's machine wears temporary white segments applied over its basic dapple finish. Note how the painter has carefully avoided obscuring any markings, all of which are still clearly visible, namely the I. *Gruppe* shield beneath the windscreen and the *Geschwader's* 'Green Heart' below the cockpit, the *Kommandeur's* chevrons, yellow fuselage theatre band (which JG 54 centred on the *Balkenkreuz*) and Eckerle's personal score on the rudder. A well-known figure on the pre-war aerobatic scene, Hauptmann Eckerle was reported missing after being forced down behind enemy lines southeast of Schlüsselburg on 14 February 1942. His final overall total of 59 earned him posthumous Oak Leaves.

27

Bf 109F-2 'White 1' of Hauptmann Reinhard Seiler, Staffelkapitän 1./JG 54, Siverskaya/Northern Sector, September 1941

This rather heavily dappled Friedrich was the mount of Reinhard Seiler, as witness both the personal emblem below the cockpit – a reminder of his days in Spain with 2./J88, the 'Top Hat' Staffel of the Legion Condor, and his nine Republican kills of the civil war – and the rudder scoreboard with his current 23 World War 2 victories (the last an I-16 downed west of Schlüsselburg on 29 September). It would require another 19 Soviet kills before Seiler was awarded the Knight's Cross on 20 December 1941, by which time he was serving as Kommandeur of III./JG 54 (see profile 30).

28

Bf 109F-4 'White 1' of Hauptmann Heinz Lange, Staffelkapitän 1./JG 54, Krasnogvardeisk/Leningrad Front, Spring 1942

Seiler's successor at the head of 1. Staffel was Oberleutnant Heinz Lange, whose late Friedrich is seen here in the 'spring thaw' colours of brown and green. Note also that Lange has reinstated the Gruppe and Geschwader badges that are so conspicuous by their absence on Seiler's machine immediately above. Lange had arrived on the Russian front with a single RAF Blenheim to his credit. And it would be a week into Barbarossa before he claimed his first Soviet kill – an Ilyushin DB-3 over Latvia. A slow but steady scorer, he was transferred late in 1942 to JG 51, with whom he achieved the last 50 of his overall total of 70 (which earned him the Knight's Cross on 18 November 1944).

29

Bf 109F-2 'Black 1' of Oberleutnant Wolfgang Späte, Staffelkapitän 5./JG 54, Staraya-Russa/Northern Sector, October 1941

Another Staffelkapitän's machine, but this time in the highly unusual and distinctive 'crazy-paving' camouflage scheme adopted by II./JG 54 during 1941. One of Germany's best-known glider pilots before the war, Wolfgang Späte had joined JG 54 in 1941 from a reconnaissance unit. Also arriving in the east with a single kill under his belt, Späte's tally quickly rose, gaining him both the Knight's Cross (on 5 October 1941 for a total of 45) and the Oak Leaves (on 23 April 1942 for 72). In mid-1942 he returned to the Reich to head the test unit developing the Me 163 rocket-fighter. And after another brief stint with JG 54 (as Kommandeur of IV. Gruppe), Späte set up JG 400 – the only Geschwader to operate the Me 163 – before ending the war flying Me 262 jets with JG 7.

30

Bf 109F-4 'White Double Chevron' of Hauptmann Reinhard Seiler, Gruppenkommandeur III./JG 54, Siverskaya/Northern Sector, Summer 1942

After serving as Staffelkapitän of 1./JG 54 (see profile 27), 'Seppl' Seiler was appointed Kommandeur of III. Gruppe on

1 October 1941, initially flying Friedrichs (as shown here), before converting to Gustavs in the late summer of 1942. Then, in mid-April 1943, he took command of I./JG 54, which was already equipped with the Fw 190. On 6 July 1943 Seiler claimed his 96th Soviet victim (taking him his tally to 100 overall), only for his own Focke-Wulf to be badly damaged in the same action east of Ponyri. Baling out severely wounded, Seiler would not return to operational flying, but spent the rest of the war in training roles, latterly as Kommodore of JG 104. He was awarded the Oak Leaves in March 1944.

31

Bf 109F-4 'Black 9' of Oberleutnant Günther Fink, 8./JG 54, Siverskaya/Northern Sector, June 1942

It was in machines such as this 'Black 9' that Günther Fink and several other pilots of JG 54 practised a rudimentary form of 'Helle Nachtjagd' (visual nightfighting) during the full-moon periods over the northern sector in the early summer of 1942. This was in addition to their normal day operations, and the Friedrichs were given no special form of night camouflage. This particular example is wearing a variation of the basic brown/green scheme (see profile 28), the only concession to its nocturnal activities being the toned-down (or simply dirty?) jettisoned fuel tank carried during the long night patrols. Nine of Fink's 56 kills came at night over the Leningrad-Volkhov fronts. III./JG 54 was transferred to Defence of the Reich duties in early 1943, and on 15 May Günther Fink, by that time a hauptmann, and Kapitän of 8. Staffel, was killed in action against US heavy bombers over the German Bight.

32

Bf 109E-7 'White 11' of Oberleutnant Horst Carganico, Staffelkapitän 1./JG 77, Petsamo/Arctic Front, July 1941

Back to the early days of Barbarossa and the Arctic front, where the only Luftwaffe fighter presence was a hybrid force of Emils and Bf 110s operating as the Jagdgruppe z.b.V. (Special-purpose fighter group). Among its component units was 1./JG 77 under Carganico, who had already claimed at least five RAF kills prior to the war with Russia. By July 1941 that total had risen to 13, as indicated on the rudder here. The latest of these (identified simply as a 'Consolidated') was most probably a GST, the Soviet licence-built version of the PBY. Early in 1942 1./JG 77 was redesignated 6./JG 5, and in April 1942 Carganico was appointed Kommandeur of II./JG 5, which he led for almost two years. Posted back to the Reich in March 1944 to assume command of I./JG 5, Carganico was killed over France on 27 May 1944.

33

Bf 109G-2 'White Chevron/Yellow 1' of Hauptmann Kurt Ubben, Gruppenkommandeur III./JG 77, Lyuban/Northern Sector, September 1942

Many of III./JG 77's machines, such as the early G-2 'gunboat' seen here, were at one time finished in very dark splinter camouflage not unlike the dark green/black-green schemes of pre-war years. Note the unusual command markings (a single white chevron combined with a yellow '1') and the impressive rudder scoreboard. Of the 84 victories recorded here, all but two have been scored on the Russian front – the last a LaGG-3 downed during a freie Jagd east of Leningrad. 'Kuddel' Ubben would claim eight more Soviet kills before III./JG 77's transfer to the Mediterranean. Appointed *Geschwaderkommodore* of JG 2 in March 1944, Major Ubben would be killed in action against P-47s the following month.

34

Bf 109F-4 'Black 13' of Oberleutnant Kurt Ubben, *Staffelkapitän* 8./JG 77, Nikolayev/Ukraine, August 1941

Prior to assuming command of III./JG 77 in September 1941, Oberleutnant Kurt Ubben had served for more than a year as *Kapitän* of 8. *Staffel*. This is his 'Black 13' towards the end of that period, the more modest rudder tally of 'only' 29 kills establishing the approximate date – his 29th victory was a Sukhoi Su-2 despatched on 17 August (and the 30th would be an I-153 fighter downed five days later). But note also the ship silhouette. Although looking like a merchantman, and positioned between aerial victories 22 and 23, this may represent the battleship HMS *Warspite*, damaged by Ubben in a fighter-bomber strike off Crete on 22 May 1941.

35

Bf 109F-4 'Black Double Chevron' of Hauptmann Anton Mader, *Gruppenkommandeur* II./JG 77, Kastornoye/Don Front, September 1942

Another high-scoring *Kommandeur* of JG 77, Mader assumed command of II. *Gruppe* a month before the start of *Barbarossa*. Arriving from JG 2, and with three kills already

to his name, he opened his Russian front scoreboard with an I-16 on 2 July 1941. By early September 1942, although the rudder here shows no sign of it, his overall total had risen to 65. After leading II./JG 77 in North Africa, Mader was selected to be the first *Geschwaderkommodore* of the newly activated JG 11 in Defence of the Reich in April 1943. He then headed JG 54 from January 1944, but his final wartime appointments are unknown.

36

Bf 109E-4 'Black Double Chevron' of Hauptmann Herbert Ihlefeld, *Gruppenkommandeur* I.(J)/LG 2, Jassy/Rumania, July 1941

With the original I./JG 77 ploughing its own furrow up in the Arctic (where it would ultimately be incorporated into JG 5), the vacant I. *Gruppe* slot with the parent JG 77 on the southern sector was filled by I.(J)/LG 2, which would itself be redesignated as the new I./JG 77 early in 1942. The long-standing *Kommandeur* of the *Gruppe*, Herbert Ihlefeld – another nine-victory Spanish Civil War *Experte* – already had 36 World War 2 kills to his credit prior to *Barbarossa*. While at the head of I.(J)/LG 2 (I./JG 77) in the east, he would elevate that overall total to 103 until, from May 1942 onwards, he was appointed *Kommodore* of a succession of other *Geschwader*, the last of them being JG 1, which he would lead for the final year of the war.

B IBLIOGRAPHY

ADERS, GEBHARD and HELD, WERNER, *Jagdgeschwader 51 Mölders*. Motorbuch Verlag, Stuttgart, 1985

BARBAS, BERND, *Planes of the Luftwaffe Fighter Aces* (2 vols.). Kookaburra, Melbourne, 1985

BRACKE, GERHARD, *Gegen vielfache Übermacht*. Motorbuch Verlag, Stuttgart, 1977

CONSTABLE, TREVOR J and TOLIVER, COL RAYMOND F (ret), *Horrido! Aces of the Luftwaffe*. Macmillan, New York, 1968

DIERICH, WOLFGANG, *Die Verbände der Luftwaffe 1935-1945*. Motorbuch Verlag, Stuttgart, 1976

EWALD, HEINZ, *Esau*. (Eigenverlag), Coburg, 1990

FAST, NIKO, *Das Jagdgeschwader 52* (various volumes). Bensberger Buch-Verlag, Bergisch Gladbach, 1990

GIRBIG, WERNER, *Jagdgeschwader 5 'Eismeerjäger'*. Motorbuch Verlag, Stuttgart, 1976

GROELER, OLAF, *Kampf um die Luftherrschaft*. Militärverlag der DDR, Berlin, 1988

HARDESTY, VON, *Red Phoenix, The Rise of Soviet Air Power, 1941-1945*. Arms and Armour Press, London, 1982

HELD, WERNER, *Die Deutschen Jagdgeschwader im Russlandfeldzug*. Podzun-Pallas-Verlag, Friedberg, 1986

HELD, WERNER, TRAUTLOFT, HANNES and BOB, EKKEHARD, *Die Grünherzjäger, Bildchronik des Jagdgeschwaders 54*. Podzun-Pallas-Verlag, Friedberg, 1985

KUROWSKI, FRANZ, *Balkenkreuz und Roter Stern, Der Lufkrieg über Russland 1941-1944*. Podzun-Pallas-Verlag, Friedberg, 1984

LIPFERT, HELMUT, *Das Tagebuch des Hauptmann Lipfert*. Motorbuch Verlag, Stuttgart, 1973

MEHNER, KURT and TEUBER, REINHARD, *Die Luftwaffe 1939-1945*. Militärverlag Klaus D Patzwall, Norderstedt, 1996

NOWARRA, HEINZ J, *Luftwaffen-Einsatz Barbarossa 1941*. Podzun-Pallas-Verlag, Friedberg

OBERMAIER, ERNST, *Die Ritterkreuzträger der Luftwaffe 1939-1945: Band I, Jagdflieger*. Verlag Dieter Hoffmann, Mainz, 1966

PIEKALKIEWICZ, JANUSZ, *Luftkrieg 1939-1945*. Südwest-Verlag, Munich, 1978

PIEKALKIEWICZ, JANUSZ, *Stalingrad, Anatomie einer Schlacht*. Südwest-Verlag, Munich

PLOCHER, Generalleutnant HERMANN, *The German Air Force versus Russia, 1942/43* (2 vols.). Arno Press, New York, 1966-67

PRIEN, JOCHEN, *Geschichte des Jagdgeschwaders 53* (3 vols.). Flugzeug (vol. 1) 1989/Struwe Druck, Eutin, 1990

PRIEN, JOCHEN, *Geschichte des Jagdgeschwaders 77* (4 vols.). Struwe Druck, Eutin, 1992

PRIEN, JOCHEN and STEMMER, GERHARD, *Jagdgeschwader 3* (4 vols. of individual Gruppe histories). Struwe Druck, Eutin

PRIEN, JOCHEN et al., *Die Jagdfliegerverbände der Deutsche Luftwaffe 1934-1945 (various vols.)*. Struwe Druck, Eutin, 2000

PRIEN, JOCHEN and RODEIKE, PETER, *Messerschmitt Bf 109F, G and K series*. Schiffer, Atglen, 1993

RALL, GÜNTHER, *Mein Flugbuch, Erinnerungen 1938-2004*. Neunundzwanzig Sechs Verlag, Moosburg, 2004

SCHERZER, VEIT, *Die Träger des Deutschen Kreuzes in Gold der Luftwaffe 1941-1945*. Scherzer's Militär Verlag, Bayreuth, 1992

SCHREIER, HANS, *JG 52*. Kurt Vowinckel-Verlag, Berg am See, 1990

SCUTTS, JERRY, *Jagdgeschwader 54 Grünherz: Aces of the Eastern Front*. Airlife, Shrewsbury, 1992

SPICK, MIKE, *Aces of the Reich: The Making of a Luftwaffe Fighter Pilot*. Greenhill Books, London, 2006

STIPDONK, PAUL and MEYER, MICHAEL, *Das Jagdgeschwader 51 (Mölders)*. VDM Heinz Nickel, Zweibrücken, 1996

INDEX